THE LENGTHENING SHADOW

by

William G. Preston

All photographs in the book are from the Davidson Companies (formerly DADCO) archives. We believe the contributors of the photos are Mic McMillon, Stuart White, Wayne Arnst, Ray Ozmon, Mat Rowley, all of Great Falls; Benham Studio, in Seattle; Marshall Noice, Kalispell' and Tim Jewett, Portland. Some photos are from unknown sources.

Front cover photo by Mic McMillan.
Back cover photo by Stuart White.

Printed in the United States of America.
10 9 8 7 6 5 4 3 2 1

Printed by Advanced Litho Printing

TO MAE:

*My best friend, partner, confidante, and critic for more than 66 years.
We have had good days and we have had bad days, but through each you
have always been there — making the bad a bit better
and the good a lot sweeter with your love and support.*

It has been a great ride!

Stanley A. Nabi, CFA

For more than 40 years, Mr. Nabi has been recognized as one of Wall Street's most distinguished economic analysts.

After graduating from Columbia University in 1954, with a degree in Economics, and completing doctoral studies at both Columbia and New York University, he joined Schweickart & Co. as an Investment Analyst. Twelve years later he left Schweickart as its Senior Managing Partner to become General Partner and Chief Investment Officer of Lazard Freres & Company.

In 1984, Mr. Nabi became Executive Vice President-Investments for Bessemer Trust Companies where he directed the investment strategy for $5.5 billion of individual and institutional assets. Since 1995, he has been Vice Chairman and Chief Investment officer of DLJ Asset Group and Chairman, Investment Policy Committee of Wood, Struthers & Winthrop, both subsidiaries of Donaldson, Lufkin & Jenrette.

He is a past president of the New York Society of Security Analysts, a former Director of the Financial Analysts Federation, and from 1971 through 1983, was an Associate Editor of the Financial Analysts Journal.

He is also an Adjunct Professor of Investment and Finance at Fordham University's Graduate School of Business, and an independent consultant to the United States Steel and Carnegie Pension Funds. As such, he is in wide demand as a lecturer and writer.

Foreword

by Stanley A. Nabi, CFA

In the early fall of 1962, at the suggestion of one of my partners, I had my first encounter with Ian B. Davidson. The purpose of the meeting was to determine whether a business relationship could be forged between our firms wherein we would represent D.A. Davidson & Co. as their "clearing agent." This, in fact, did come to pass. It also gave birth to an admiring friendship based on trust and common interest.

At the time, the firm in which I was a partner held seats on the New York Stock Exchange, acted as a "specialist" on the American Stock Exchange and the Pacific Coast Stock Exchange, and was a member of several other stock and commodity exchanges. Among the other functions it performed was that of being a "correspondent" for other firms, settling their trades with other stock brokers and providing various administrative services.

My first impression of Ian can be summed up in a few adjectives, none of which typically describe those who held the reins in the investment community in New York then or since. He was quiet but not timid, polite to a fault, deferential and understated. In the absence of any information on his academic training and professional experience, his gentle demeanor could easily have been confused for a shortage of ability or competence.

Wall Street has always been a place where egos rule supreme, aggressiveness is mistaken for determination, success is measured by the results of the latest transaction, and self-promotion is the stepping stone to bigger things. Measured against these unappealing yardsticks, Ian fell quite short.

As my partners and I outlined the services offered by our firm, Ian listened intently taking no written notes but obviously absorbing the details being proffered. When the time came for him to elicit information, his questions were direct, relevant, piercing and succinct. This was a man in command of his subject matter, displaying a keen interest in all aspects of the business, from simple administrative functions to investment research and product development. Most revealing, however, were his plans for growing D.A. Davidson & Co. His strategy was measured, disciplined and as low risk as any I have encountered in more than forty years in the investment business.

As Ian outlined his vision of the future of the Davidson firm, several guideposts emerged, all of which he held with strong conviction. First, he sought to build a firm whose attributes mirrored the character of the community it serves. In Montana, this implied a conservative, value-minded, defensive approach. Second, he concluded, quite correctly, that trust is a key factor in providing investment services, and trust can only be earned by placing customers and their interests first. This could only be achieved by developing an intimate knowledge of the client, his business, his family structure and his long-term financial needs and goals. Third, he realized that he could not round the circle without surrounding himself with professionals who shared his vision, his temperament, and his commitments.

A trip to Montana in April of 1963, the first of nearly forty that I would undertake since then, was far more revealing than I could have possibly imagined. My impression of the state had been gathered from reading about the "Wild West" which made me imagine that the investment personnel that I would encounter would be cowboys with a limited command of their subject matter. I was quickly disabused of this embarrassing arrogance.

Upon my arrival on a Saturday morning at the modest Davidson office in Great Falls, all of the investment executives were hard at work either counseling clients, reading investment literature or performing administrative tasks beyond the call of their duties. Though better read and informed than nearly all of their counterparts in the large financial centers of the country, they were quick to express concern that they suffered from not being at the leading edge of the information pipeline. To bridge this imaginary gap, they clearly summoned the extra effort required to excel. It soon became obvious that history, geography and culture had spawned a sense of value, a feeling of responsibility, and a devotion to community that provided a map for how life is lived and how to foster personal relationships based on mutual trust and respect.

By the early 1960s, the post-war explosion in "People's Capitalism," generational changes in perceptions and attitudes, and the gradual dissolution of the morbid fear of another depression were giving way to explosive growth on Wall Street as prosperity generated wealth. Old firms expanded by opening offices in cities and towns whose culture they did not comprehend and by introducing new products whose risks they did not or could not accurately measure. Structured mainly as limited partnerships, their capital was transitory, exiting at will and often when needed most. Risk assessment was rarely a serious pursuit, given mere lip service, if considered at all. By the end of the decade, the growth of the securities business was nearly running out of control, causing many illustrious, long-established firms to disappear, liquidate or merge out of existence.

Each market cycle has claimed its own victims as the nature of the business evolved from the simple process of dealing in stocks and bonds to one whose global reach, complexity, and multitude of products have created a web beyond the simple human mind to master. The speed of modern communications has made markets far more efficient but inherently more fraught with risks. A transaction that at any specific moment may seem to provide an opportunity for significant profits can reverse course in a nanosecond as the smallest of computers telegraph its potential and level the playing field.

By the early 1970s, regulatory and other changes had spawned a highly competitive global industry with cross-border risks which had often proven difficult to manage or control. In addition, the industry had become so impersonal that it was executing and processing tens of millions of transactions daily with none of the players interfacing, or having the slightest familiarity with those involved on the other side of a trade. The proliferation of products and services offered had multiplied to an extent that many of them become indistinguishable from each other, and were so difficult to comprehend that they drove the average investor to extreme confusion and frustration. This, in brief, is the business climate in which D.A. Davidson & Co. has managed to expand and prosper.

Ian Davidson's soothing approach to personal relationships came through loud and clear when I met his father, David Davidson, the founder of the firm who guided its destiny during the dark days of the Great Depression. Conservative in his political and social views, fearless in personal demeanor, Dave did not shrink from expressing his strongly held beliefs no matter the consequences. In a business where personal interaction and relaxed exchanges are critical requisites, he came across as one who perceived his well-earned reputation for integrity and high moral principles as the end rather than the beginning of a relationship. Given Ian's gentle demeanor, it was logical for those not familiar with his inner strength to question whether father and son could function together in harmony. The outcome was a case study for modern psychologists. Both sides retained their individuality by playing down differences in their styles which could have impeded their common effort to build the firm. Such low key, nonconfrontational approach has remained a constant Davidson mantra, building on common interests while gradually bridging differences.

Personal recollections aside, I have often reflected on the consistency of the Davidson firm's growth, notably how it managed to safeguard the character of its business without in any way compromising its objectives. A primary purpose of this examination was to determine whatever there were lessons to be learned or strategies that can be copied or adapted.

Success alone rarely provides a useful outline or an efficient guide. In an industry known for its hyperboles, success is often measured by the outcome of a single event, or within a very brief timespan, rather than by the staying power through periods of highs and lows. In the case of D.A. Davidson & Co., its growth has lasted more than four decades of turbulent times and wrenching changes for its industry and emerged as a strong, vital institution.

Perhaps the most notable part of the journey was that it began with modest goals rather than a grand design loaded with inflexible objectives, faulty assumptions, and exaggerated expectations. These objectives were fashioned so that they could be easily attained using available resources, talent, the best of intentions, and the good will of community and clients. The wisdom in this approach early on provided the philosophical and fundamental foundation that defined all subsequent efforts. Given the conservative bent of the community and the market the firm planned to serve, this was a wise decision. It telegraphed a message of emotional reciprocity that generated empathy and comfort all around. If the firm providing service and advice is conducting its own affairs in a prudent, conservative manner, it was reasoned that it would do the same for its clients.

At the root of investing as a discipline is a simple principle which is frequently cited but rarely heeded. Successful investing is nothing more than a method by which a risk-adjusted fair rate of return is obtained over an extended period. This goal is eminently attainable, but it can only be achieved in a climate of consistency in which the ability and willingness to take risks are objectively defined. In pursing the expansion plans for the firm, Ian Davidson was a strict adherent to this principle. Each step forward was first evaluated for risk before the seductive smell of its potential rewards was allowed to intoxicate. No giant gambles were considered in the search for glory, and a "fall back" strategy was always at hand to be implemented quickly and at minimal cost, if necessary. Furthermore, needed capital to finance the expansion had to be internally generated rather than borrowed, while the support system was frequently upgraded and tested to make sure that the safety and integrity of the chain of service would not be compromised. Building a skyscraper on a framehouse foundation, which caused the downfall of many firms, was never treated as an option.

Throughout its years of growth, the firm has always maintained an active involvement in community affairs. Even today, many clients recall the investment seminars of the earlier years that turned into social as well as educational events and that were attended by guests who traveled

A Davidson Investment Seminar in Butte headlined by Stanley Nabi.

long distances. These seminars have continued for more than 35 years, frequently supplemented by media presentations by senior analysts and investment experts. Although some may view the effort as a marketing tool, their main purpose is to connect the community with sources of information available in other financial centers around the country. That the firm's policy encourages active leadership in community projects is also reflected in the wide participation by a long list of executives and employees in civic, educational, and religious affairs. In the most practical terms, such involvement provides valuable lessons in understanding the changes, needs, and the mindset as well as the generational progression of clients.

Wherever the Davidson firm is represented, it consciously made itself an extension of the community it serves. In a form of cultural exchange, the community has always been willing to return this favor with immense benefits to both sides. Despite having built national recognition, this climate of mutual trust has provided the professional justification to remain a regional firm. This key decision has served to eliminate the excessive risks typically associated with aggressive growth at the peak of the bull market cycle as well as the extreme uncertainty inherent in globalization.

No business can prosper for long without the loyalty, support and enthusiasm of its employees. Failure is assured if those who toil daily are made to feel as if they are cogs in a machine rather than as worthy participants, even partners, in the common pursuit of excellence. From its early days of expansion, the Davidson template included promotions to managerial positions from within. As an extension of this policy, it has encouraged qualified offsprings of employees to join the firm. It has spread the fruits of success by providing executives with an opportunity to become equity holders through a variety of incentive programs. Such a close and admiring relationship was quite evident a few years ago at one of the outings sponsored by the firm to which I was invited. In a magnificent display worthy of envy, Ian Davidson was able to recall the name of every employee present as well as that of their spouse, list the number of children in the family and, in some cases, the hobbies in which they participated. A greater affirmation of inclusion could not have been better displayed. This approach to relations extends well beyond name recognition. Achievement is promptly and quietly recognized but is not permitted to create a corrosive climate of hostility, envy or destructive competition.

If the foregoing, together with the contents of this book, appears to dwell on Ian Davidson and the firm he was instrumental in building into a leading institution within a rapidly changing industry, it is because the two are inextricably bonded with a glue which is part vision, part determination, and part philosophy and culture. The roots planted have become so well-entrenched and secure that there is no cause for concern that people or events might radically alter a winning formula. Ian— coach, cheerleader, gentle critic—and a meticulously selected crew of talented senior executives remain the guardians of a heritage they created and nurtured. Andrew Davidson, long in training and with many of the personal qualities that served his father well, may some day carry the torch, if he so chooses.

No better reflection of the history and constancy of the Davidson firm could be had than the evolution of the complex which currently houses its headquarters in Great Falls. From a modest storefront forty years ago, located on the street floor in the present location, it has been expanded in small steps, nearly brick by brick, into the magnificent structure which has become the established center and architectural focus of the business district. It stands as a metaphor for the successful approach to investing practiced by the firm and its executives — plan for the long-term but in measured steps, objectively assess the trade-off between risk and reward, apply the best tools of the profession, shun greed and opportunism, and the final results should prove a source of satisfaction and justifiable pride.

William G. Preston

BILL PRESTON IS A NATIVE MONTANAN. EDUCATED IN GREAT FALLS PUBLIC SCHOOLS AND AT THE UNIVERSITY OF WASHINGTON, HE BECAME AN AGENT IN HIS FATHER'S AGENCY OF NORTHWESTERN NATIONAL LIFE INSURANCE COMPANY IN 1933. UPON HIS FATHER'S DEATH IN 1942, HE BECAME THE MANAGER OF THE AGENCY. IN 1950, THE AGENCY WAS EXPANDED TO INCLUDE THE ENTIRE STATE, AND BILL WAS NAMED MONTANA MANAGER OF NWNL.

IN 1954, BILL WAS ASKED TO RELOCATE TO MINNEAPOLIS TO HEAD THE NWNL HOME OFFICE AGENCY ... THE COMPANY'S LARGEST. HE HELD THE POSITION UNTIL 1970 WHEN HE RESIGNED TO ESTABLISH FINANCIAL AIMS CORPORATION, A FINANCIAL PLANNING AND ASSET MANAGEMENT ORGANIZATION.

FINANCIAL AIMS WAS ACQUIRED IN 1975 BY D.A. DAVIDSON & CO. AND ITS HEADQUARTERS RELOCATED TO GREAT FALLS. BILL WAS RETAINED AS PRESIDENT. IT IS NOW ONE OF THE DADCO COMPANIES.

BILL RETIRED FROM FAC IN 1981, BUT HAS REMAINED WITH THE COMPANY AS A CONSULTANT TO DADCO. HE AND MAE, HIS WIFE OF 66 YEARS, CONTINUE TO MAKE THEIR HOME IN GREAT FALLS WHERE HE STILL MAINTAINS AN ACTIVE INTEREST IN COMMUNITY AFFAIRS. IN 1982, HE SERVED AS A MEMBER OF THE GOVERNOR'S COUNCIL ON MANAGEMENT AT THE INVITATION OF MONTANA'S THEN-GOVERNOR, TED SCHWINDEN.

Prologue

by William G. Preston

The idea of writing the story of DADCO has been a long time in the making. The seed was sown shortly after I retired from Financial Aims in 1982. I started to think back on my relatively short experience with what was then D.A. Davidson & Co. I became fascinated with the firm's unique history and with the message that history seemed to convey about free enterprise and democracy. It seemed to me that most of the principles embodied in the DADCO culture were also those which made the free market system in America different from what passed for free enterprise as it is actually practiced elsewhere in the world.

The idea germinated slowly. It was nourished from time to time by Stanley Nabi and others. I stayed on after formal retirement in a consultative capacity, with a desk next to Ian Davidson's office, where I was able to watch the ebb and flow of activity as it passed by me. I also became acquainted with many state and national leaders, both within and without the securities industry, who increasingly sought out Ian Davidson and other DADCO officials as the company grew in size and influence. My volunteer work with the DADCO *Exchange,* its quarterly employee publication, afforded me the opportunity to become acquainted with the background and the personal data of many of the people of DADCO, old-timers and newcomers—their history, their achievements, and their personal triumphs and tragedies. It transformed my picture of DADCO from that of a successful business organization to one of a team of skilled and highly-motivated individuals working together in harmony to reach a common goal and having fun and finding personal satisfaction in the doing.

At the outset, I was not sure I was the one best suited to tell the story. After all, Ian Davidson was a part of our family. He had been unconditionally accepted as a family member when he married our daughter, Nancy; and the better we knew him, the more our love for him as a person, and our admiration for him as a business executive, grew. Since any story about DADCO is inextricably intertwined with that of Ian Davidson, whatever I wrote about either might be perceived as biased and colored by our personal relationship. That, I must confess, is understandable skepticism. I love the guy—and admire him immensely ... and this from a father-in-law!

My hesitance was further heightened by the lack of enthusiasm with which Ian greeted the idea when first approached. He abhors anything that smacks of personal aggrandizement. His first reaction was a concern that people would perceive it as an ego trip on his part. I was sensitive to his concerns. However, it appeared that if the story was to be told, I was likely the only one with both time and interest to undertake the task. I felt strongly that it was a story worth telling. Not only is it a unique and outstanding example of American entrepreneurship in action, but it also conveys a message that seems to be missing in much of today's permissive society: Character does count; and integrity, honesty, and fair-dealing carry with them their own rewards. As one of the best teachers I encountered in all of my educational experience was fond of reminding her classes: "Honesty is not only the best policy, it is the only one that truly counts."

So, with assurances that we would respect his concerns, and give due credit to others for the part they played, Ian agreed to furnish such information as only he could provide to allow us to tell an accurate story.

Important as Ian Davidson's part in the building of DADCO has been, it certainly has not been a one-man show. He has been aided, assisted—and, in many cases guided - by a host of talented and dedicated people, only a few of whom are we able to acknowledge with more than a passing reference and still keep our story to a readable length. But possibly the greatest tribute we can pay to Ian Davidson is that he has been able to attract such people to his cause, instill in them enthusiasm for the DADCO culture, and meld them into a cohesive team, committed to a common goal. It is true leadership in its purest form.

Despite my initial reluctance, I felt that I did bring to the project a background of experience that would enable me to give it a fair measure of unbiased objectivity. For more than 40 years, a major part of my work was to select new sales personnel for a major life insurance company, and to see that those chosen received the education and training they needed to do their job. During that time, I administered scores of aptitude tests, conducted dozens of screening interviews with prospective new personnel, and played an active part in the training of those chosen. I discovered that there were certain qualities shared by those who were successful that were lacking to a greater or lesser degree in those who were not.

My participation in industry organizations afforded me the chance to become personally acquainted with some of the most successful executives in the business. I made it a point to try to learn some of the reasons for their success. The experience enabled me to make better choices in my own process of selection and training. I came to know what to look for and how to evaluate the importance of the attributes which the people I interviewed could bring to the job we needed to fill.

I had started a business of my own from scratch and had the personal experience of shepherding it through all the problems of gestation to the point where it became a viable cog in a growing conglomerate of diversified financial services.

These experiences enabled me to recognize—and better understand and appreciate—the superb display of leadership and teamwork I saw at work as I sat in my little corner and watched new records set year after year with almost monotonous regularity.

I also had the advantage of having lived through many of the events of history to which I have referred. The impact on the lives of those who lived through them are still vividly etched in my memory.

Both Harry and Charlie Davidson had been personal friends long before I became acquainted with their nephew, Ian. Harry's essays on the early history of the Davidson family were of inestimable value in assessing the kind of people they were and what make them tick as a family. He was a special friend, while Charlie Davidson was responsible for my receiving a personal recognition which I still cherish. Ian's mother was a friend of my wife long before Ian became our son-in-law.

We go back a long way with the Davidson family, whom we knew and admired before there was any thought of a family relationship.

Few important undertakings are accomplished single-handedly. It has taken the individual contributions of many people to bring DADCO to its present position of pre-eminence in its niche. In like manner, there have been a lot of people who have helped in the writing of this story. To all who have contributed with their enthusiasm, their encouragement, and their personal recollections, we extend our heartfelt gratitude. It has made the project exciting and challenging. Specifically, we would single out Johan Miller, Bill Macfadden, Gene Hufford, Bev and Bob Braig, Bruce Madsen, Stu Nicholson, Charlie Abernathy, Vinney Purpura, and Charlie Bowers for their recollections and observations in regard to the early history of D.A. Davidson & Co. They all played a significant role in establishing it on a solid foundation for its subsequent growth. Their personal contributions added much to make it a story about real human beings and not just a collection of historical data.

We also owe a debt of profound gratitude to LaVonne Harp, Ian's "gal Friday" and computer whiz extraordinaire, for her help in typing and editing, re-typing and re-editing, the manuscript and preparing it for publication. Without her devotion to this project for lo' these many months, it is doubtful it would have ever gotten off the ground.

Our thanks to Butch Larcombe and Stacey Suydam of DADCO for their editing help and constructive suggestions; to Terry Cady and all the gang at Advanced Litho for their super production job; to Debbie Rhodes for her graphic design work; and finally, to Stanley Nabi for his foreword and his encouragement over many years.

Without all of them, none of this would have taken place.

Table of Contents

THE LENGTHENING SHADOW

PART I

Setting the Stage

As I write this, there are exactly 100 days remaining in the 20th Century. There will be even fewer by the time you read it. Our count assumes that you accept December 31, 1999, as the century's last day. If you are one who argues for January 1, 2001 as the official start of the 21st Century, add another 366 days. (2000 is a leap year!)

In either case, it seems a certainty, correctly or not, that January 1, 2000, will, in fact, usher in a new millennium—and millions of people around the globe will use the occasion as an excuse for a wild celebration.

It is a response typical of the times in which we live.

... And what a century it has been! At its dawning, our nation had just taken its first tentative step into the international arena. The Monroe Doctrine, decreeing that the Americas—North and South—were off limits for colonizing by foreign powers, had been a declared national policy for almost a century. Yet, Spain's foray into Cuba in 1898 was its first serious challenge.

America successfully repelled the challenge. Still, it was hesitant to accept the responsibilities of leadership. It seemed to be unsure that it really wanted to become a world power. The ambivalence persisted through World War I and well into the Roosevelt years. It took three years for our leaders to decide it was our national duty to get involved in World War I to, as Woodrow Wilson described it: "...make the world safe for democracy." After it did so, it again had second thoughts. Congress rejected Wilson's plea to become a member of the League of Nations. Then, in 1930, Congress enacted the Smoot-Hawley Tariff Act in a desperate effort to jump-start a stalled economy after the stock market crash in 1929.

Historians cite these two actions—the rejection of membership in

David A. Davidson

the League of Nations and the Smoot-Hawley Tariff Act—as major contributors to the worldwide economic collapse that followed World War I. It set the stage for the rise of Adolph Hitler and World War II. Yet it was not until it appeared that a Nazi reign of terror might engulf all of Europe, and the Japanese launched a sneak attack on Pearl Harbor, that America finally concluded that, if the ideal of individual freedom for all was to survive and grow, our country had to accept the mantle of world leadership which had been thrust upon it. It was not an easy sell. In the 1920s, Joseph Stalin began to solidify his brand of totalitarian communism, first in the Soviet Union, then by export to its neighbors. A threat from Nazi Germany to Soviet survival forced Stalin to join forces with the United States and its democratic allies in World War II. As soon as the shooting ended, however, a Cold War state of military uneasiness resumed. It lasted until the dramatic collapse of communism in 1990. During the interim, military involvement, first in Korea, then in Vietnam, spawned civil unrest at home. It resulted in the first outright military defeat for the United States in its history.

Even as this is written, freedom for the people in Bosnia and Kosovo is under attack from Serbia; in Iraq from Saddam Hussein; and in Iran from its theocratic mullahs. In each, its peoples look to America for help—help that debates in Congress indicate some national leaders are still reluctant to give.

America is learning that the cost of leadership is indeed steep.

While this was being played out on the stage of international politics, much was also happening on other fronts.

As the 20th Century opened, the country was still coping with the fallout from the Civil War. That conflict had irrevocably cemented a divided nation into one political entity, but it was still far from united. Slavery had been officially abolished, but racial tolerance and universal freedom existed in name only. The century would be more than half spent before Rosa Parks ushered in the Civil Rights movement when she refused to surrender her seat on a bus in 1955. Thanks to Martin Luther King, Jr., and others like him, much progress has been made on this front; but it is far from an accomplished fact as we greet 2000 and the new century.

As it has been from the dawn of time, economics was a dominant force in the 20th Century. Fueled by a myriad of amazing technologies, many of them inspired by the exigencies of war and by a burgeoning explosion in population, America has moved from a predominately domestic agrarian economy to a sophisticated inter-continental industrial conglomerate. By the end of the century, agriculture accounted for barely 5% of the gross domestic product. As a result, a host of serious social problems, as well as drastic economic dislocations, have occupied much of its attention for a major part of the century.

World War I had barely ground to a halt when the country was hit with a catastrophic epidemic of influenza, followed a decade later by an economic depression of unprecedented proportions. The flu epidemic was particularly shattering. Though its devastation has been overshadowed in history by the toll from two world wars, the flu epidemic of 1918 ranks as the single most deadly event of the 20th Century. To put its ravage in proper perspective, figures from the World Almanac report that fewer than 700,000 Americans have died in the last 100 years from all wars—WWI, WWII, Korea, Vietnam, and Desert Storm—as well as from all acts of terrorism involving Americans. Yet, in less than a six-month period starting late in 1918, the same source tells us that 548,000 men, women and children died from influenza. Scarcely a family was spared its call, as those few of us still alive who lived through it can vividly remember.

As the decade of the '20s opened, the country shook off the effects of epidemic and depression. Domestic rebuilding became the order of the day. There was much to be done to meet the backlog of unfulfilled needs and wants which the war had put on hold. These combined to create unprecedented demands on the American economy. It engendered a false sense of security. The country went on an euphoric economic binge. People discovered the stock market. It seemed a sure way to get rich without effort. Anyone who was anyone "played the market." Stories abounded of cab drivers and waitresses making a killing through tips dropped, deliberately or inadvertently, by customers reputed to have confidential inside knowledge. Man's timeless quest for the mythical pot of gold seemed, finally, to have been realized until a fateful day in October 1929 when it all came crashing down. It ushered in the Great Depression.

Few today have any real comprehension of what the economic climate was like in the 1930s. The Great Depression tore asunder the fragile underpinnings of a nation which had only begun to regain its economic vitality after a bloody war in Europe to rescue a foreign people from an arrogant militaristic oligarchy. At the depression's height, one of every four employable persons in the country were unable to find work—any work! The first act of the first presidency of Franklin Delano Roosevelt was to close every bank in America to forestall a threatened collapse of the nation's banking system. Some four out of every ten of them never reopened. The first tentative steps had just been taken to monitor and regulate the nation's financial markets. It was a voyage into uncharted waters. No one yet had any clear vision of where they would lead.

I vividly recall a personal experience from that day. I lived in a fraternity house at college with some fifteen other students. The day the banks closed, we gathered to inventory our cash assets. Among the entire group, we could raise less than $50. Ironically, that morning I had received a small check from my mother. It was worthless. Her bank was closed, as was every bank where I might cash it.

It was an experience which I have never forgotten.

For better or for worse, the Great Depression of the 1930s forever changed America, its institutions, and its way of life.

Such was the economic climate on October 14, 1935, when David Adams Davidson, a Montana banker, opened a retail stock brokerage office in Great Falls, Montana. The event was notable only because of the prevailing economic conditions of the time. It was an act of great daring and courage. In 1935, most businesses were trying to keep from failing, not daring to start something new. The 1929 crash of the stock market, together with the bank closures in 1932, had shattered the faith of the American people in the integrity of its financial institutions as had no other occurrence, before or since.

These problems were compounded for Dave by the recent closure of the only remaining stock brokerage in Great Falls. Normally, that might have been an asset. It eliminated all local competition. In Dave's case, however, it only added to the prevailing climate of distrust. The firm had closed under a cloud of suspicion, fueled by charges of unethical and unlawful financial manipulations. Disillusioned customers had lost much of their savings. They were bitter about their experience and distrustful of anything that had to do with the stock market. The prevailing feeling was captured in a statement by a prominent business man in the community and reported by Dave's brother, Harry, in a booklet about the Davidson family written for private family distribution: "I like Dave and I trust him, but I lost a lot of money in those other brokerage firms, and I wouldn't put a damn cent in any of them—not even Dave's!"

The Lengthening Shadow is the story of the business which David Adams Davidson started in 1935. He is the DAD in D.A. Davidson & Co. An inside company joke is that they are grateful that George chose *Adams*, not *Ulysses,* for his son's middle name, else the firm might have been a *DUD* instead of a *DAD.* It is a business, born in the depths of the most violent economic cataclysm the country has ever known; surviving through three major wars and a world-wide social revolution; and come to full flower in the final third of the 20th Century to become a dominant force in the securities industry in the region in which it has chosen to operate.

It is a story which, far from ended, has, in the opinion of many, only begun.

Actually, this book tells two separate, but related, stories: that about the firm then known as Gibson Associates that existed before the arrival of Ian Bruce Davidson; and that about DADCO, the firm it became after his arrival. The first is a story of survival, where its reputation in the community was established, and the tone set for its future modus operandi. The second is the story of a commitment to a vision and inspired leadership which transformed that vision into a dynamic reality.

We have two reasons for telling this story.

The first, and most obvious, is to recognize and pay tribute to the principal players in this real-life drama, to their vision and commitment to excellence which gave them the courage to seize an opportunity to serve a public need in a society in chaos. Though the industry in which Dave Davidson chose to start his business had been wracked with excesses ranging from unreasonable expectations to outright fraud, he knew that investing in the growth of American business was vital, not only to the recovery of its economy, but to its long-term prosperity. He knew that the business climate in the community which he chose was one rife with suspicion and distrust of anything financial. Yet he believed that the people of Montana deserved the chance to share in the future prosperity of America which he was confident would come.

He also had faith that his reputation for honesty and fair dealing, and his acknowledged expertise in matters financial, would overcome the suspicion and distrust arising from past actions of others. He was confident that he could build a successful business based on putting the welfare of its customers first in all its future dealings. This was the governing credo on which D.A. Davidson opened a branch office in Great Falls for E.J. Gibson, Inc. in 1935. It is the credo which governs its successor, the DADCO Companies, today.

The first office was housed in what is now the lobby entrance of the modern five-story Davidson Building in downtown Great Falls. At the time, it was a one-story Steele Building. Mr. Davidson's office was located in the space now occupied by the building's two elevators. The story of its transformation from Steele to Davidson is the subject of a later chapter.

Dave Davidson's gamble was modestly successful. It provided a modest living for himself and a secretary from its opening in 1935 until 1958 when his son, Ian Bruce Davidson, joined forces with him. It is what has happened since that is the heart and soul of the message it contains for any who harbor a desire to start a new enterprise, or to expand or change the direction of an existing one.

This leads to the second reason to tell the Davidson story.

For much of the Twentieth Century, an undeclared—but very real—state of economic cold war has tacitly existed between the public sector

The Steele Building housed the first D.A. Davidson & Co. office, pictured are David A. Davidson and Ian B. Davidson in 1960.

represented by government, and the private sector, represented by business. The conflict was born in such displays of corporate greed as that practiced by the Standard Oil Company which attempted to gain a monopoly through a system of interlocking ownerships; and by the Teapot Dome scandals of the Harding years where bribes to public officials were the road to economic preference. It was nurtured by the politics of Franklin Roosevelt's New Deal which pitted the poor against the well-to-do and exploited their differences in economic status for political advantage. It has grown into a full-blown chasm between those who believe that government should be a facilitator to those who want to own and run their own affairs, and those who see government as a benevolent dictator, policing the activities of the private sector for what it perceives to be the greater benefit of society. Much of the legislative and judicial activity since the days of the Great Depression has been an attempt to bridge the chasm.

No business—public or private—will endure if it does not meet some human need or desire. It was Sir Winston Churchill who once commented that democracy is the world's most inefficient form of government except when compared with all the rest. Free enterprise is like that. Run by people obsessed by a lust for power or greed, it can create labor strife, public distrust, and shoddy products. Yet, compared with the brutality of Germany's National Socialism, or the ruthless exploitation of Soviet Communism, or variations thereof by other societies, America's system based on free enterprise still stands as the world's most vibrant economy, offering more freedom and opportunity to more of its people than any system yet devised.

Virtually all the great economic success stories in the last half century in America have been written by visionaries with an idea—and the courage and will to pursue them. Microsoft, Wal-Mart, Nordstrom's, Southwest Airlines are but a few of the hundreds of such enterprises providing thousands of new jobs and millions of dollars in new wealth. None of these existed at the start of the 20th Century.

DADCO—a highly successful business in the fiercely-competitive, but somewhat mundane, field of financial services—belongs on the list. It is a business which depends on a high level of technical sophistication, yet is located in one of the most unlikely places in the country in which to establish and maintain such an enterprise. Its story is a study of leadership style which inspires people, in whatever capacity they serve, to do their best by making them feel important. It is a story of a vision of the kind of organization its architects aspired to build; and of their steadfast commitment to time-tested principles of honesty, integrity, and common sense as cornerstones of the structure they built. It is a story of careful planning, hard work, triumph, and tragedy.

It is a story that is quintessential Americana. That means that it is an example of the best that America's free enterprise system can produce. It was born in the economic chaos of the Great Depression—and survived. It came to maturity in the social revolution of the Vietnam years—and prospered. Now, as a new millennium is about to begin, it finds itself about to realize—it if has not already done so—the dream it dreamed almost a half century ago to become the pre-eminent firm in its field in the region in which it has chosen to conduct its activities.

How it was done—and why—and who was involved is the subject of this story. If, from its recitation, others glean some ideas which will enable them to better realize their own dream, everyone will be a winner. May it be so.

It's in the Genes

Our story begins in Dundee, Scotland in 1901 when George Davidson, a tenter in a burlap factory, was advised by his doctor to move his family to a more friendly climate in America. His wife suffered from a serious lung condition; the dank and damp Scottish weather was a handicap to her recovery. Mrs. Davidson's brother, David Craig, had migrated to the United States some years earlier. He settled in Conrad, Montana, and sent back glowing reports about the opportunities which abounded in that semi-arid western climate. Burlap workers in Scotland could barely support their families, let alone save enough to fund a trip for a family of six to America. So, when he learned of his sister's condition, Mr. Craig offered to advance the money for their trip to Great Falls.

A glimpse into the character of George Davidson is found in the booklet written by Harry Davidson, his oldest son: "... and it might be added that the advance was paid back in small payments as soon as possible."

So it was that on July 4, 1901, George Davidson, his wife, Isabella,

George Davidson and family during WWI.

and their four children, Edith, Harry, Charles and David, set sail from Glasgow, Scotland for the United States.

The move was successful. Mrs. Davidson recovered, outlived her husband by nearly ten years, and died in 1953 at the age of 90.

In his booklet, Harry recounts details of the family's trip to Montana, the poverty they endured, and the problems they encountered in adjusting to new surroundings. It is a story of deep devotion to family; of willingness to accept personal responsibility without complaint or bitterness; of pride in performing whatever task they were assigned to the very best of their ability; and of uncompromising integrity in all their dealings with others. It was undergirded by an unshakable, yet humble, religious faith in the omnipotence of God and in the essential goodness of their fellow human beings. They did not "wear their faith on their sleeve." They simply lived it without apology; at the same time respecting those with whom they might differ in theology or form.

Harry summed it up this way: "I have never known a better man than my Dad. He was a wonderful influence on the life of all of us."

That was the heritage bequeathed to David Adams Davidson, founder of the original DADCO company which bears his name.

No story about Ian Davidson and the building of DADCO would be complete, however, without a special reference to his mother, Florence Scott Davidson—universally and affectionately known as "Scottie." She spent her entire working life as an elementary school teacher, with time out only to raise two boys. (A third son died in infancy.) Ian's brother, David, a prominent Montana architect who bears his father's name, favored his father in looks, personality, and demeanor more than did Ian. D.A. Davidson was, in the words of his brother, "...a very conservative man in every way; in business, in political opinions, even in dress." In his early banking career, he was the victim of a closure of two banks in which he held minor positions. In the early 1920s, such failures were common. In another case he was falsely charged, by association, with wrong-doing. These incidents, Harry wrote, "left their mark on Dave...making him withdraw into himself, thus adding to his natural conservatism."

Scottie Davidson, on the other hand, was a "people" person. She was almost revered by many of her former students who, over the course of the 40-odd years she taught in Great Falls, rose to positions of prominence in the community and the state. She was a superb teacher with a warmth and self-confidence not easily detected in the dour Scottish bearing of her husband.

Her devotion to her community and country was exemplified by her record of public service. For many years she teamed up with her lawyer brother-in-law, Charles Davidson, to conduct classes in Americanism for those applying for U.S. citizenship. Together, they prepared hundreds of new immigrants to become useful and knowledgeable citizens of their chosen new land.

Those who knew the Davidson family well often referred to the older boy as "Dave's son," while Ian was usually "Scottie's boy." Thus it is somewhat ironic that it was Ian who joined his father in 1958 in his struggling stock brokerage business.

In hindsight, Ian's decision to cast his lot with his father seems to have been not only a consequence of his heritage, but almost an inevitable occurrence. But it was not made without a certain amount of trepidation and soul searching. Both as a family member and as a result of his research for an MBA thesis, he was well aware of the firm's uncertain future. At J.A. Hogle & Co. where he was then employed, he had a modest but stable income base and a bright future with an established company. He had also made some influential friends in high places in the academic field. So it was not without an element of personal risk that he chose to return to Great Falls to help his father turn Gibson Associates around and change the direction of its future.

It was what he had been preparing himself for since his early college days. In his genes were the warmth of his mother's love of people and the Scottish conservatism and independence of his father.

It was a fortuitous combination for success.

David S., Scottie, David A. and Ian in front of the family home, 1943.

Ian Davidson and his father, David, in the early 1950s.

Acorns and Oaks

According to an old proverb: "Great oaks from little acorns grow." The English gentry who confronted King John in the meadows of Runneymede in 1215 probably had no historic political agenda in mind. They sought only to redress some grievous wrongs they had endured at the hands of authority run amok. But the resulting Magna Charta set the tone for the entire system of English jurisprudence for all the centuries which have followed.

It is also unlikely that the diverse conglomerate of soldiers, lawyers, merchants, and farmers who met in Philadelphia in 1787 to "... form a more perfect union, establish justice, and insure domestic tranquillity ..." deliberately set out to produce a document which William Gladstone, the great prime minister of Great Britain, once called "the most wonderful work ever struck at a given time by the brain and purpose of man." Yet the Constitution of the United States is the longest lasting national constitution in the world today.

In like manner, when Ian Davidson wrote a thesis on "The Potential of a Small, Single-Office Investment Firm" as a requirement for an MBA degree from the University of California-Berkeley in July 1956, he could not know that he was producing the basic blueprint for the systematic growth and development of what is, today, the largest and arguably the most respected regional securities firm in the Pacific Northwest. Yet, it was the foundation of a vision, sketched in surprisingly complete detail as an academic exercise, and fleshed out over the years which followed in the cauldron of intense real-life competition.

Ian Davidson was a product of the American public school system. Early in his schooling, his competitive drive and his desire to excel showed itself in his love of sports. Unfortunately, his physical attributes did not lend themselves to great athletic prowess. He was short in stature and slight of build, typical of the Davidson clan, but not the stuff of which great linebackers or gifted guards are made. This did not deter him, however. In high school he was the team manager in football, basketball, and track in all four of his high school years. An omen of things to come was this accolade in his high school graduation yearbook from Bill Swarthout, his football coach: "I don't know what we will do without you next year. We'll miss you more than our ball players."

His interest in sports has endured. He rarely misses a Grizzly football game at his beloved University of Montana. The luxury Davidson box at Washington-Grizzly Stadium is heavily used by DADCO people for employee and public relations purposes.

Nancy and Ian were among the hundreds of loyal U of M fans in the stands at Huntington, West Virginia in 1995 and 1996 to watch their Grizzlies compete for the National Division II-A football championship. (They won one and lost one.)

Following his high school graduation, Ian attended the University of Montana, receiving a B.A. degree in Accounting in 1953. He also enrolled in the R.O.T.C. program which provided some financial help in return for a stint in military service after graduation. The war in Korea was still in full swing. He chose the Air Force and, upon graduation, was commissioned a second lieutenant with orders to report to Lowery Air Force Base in Denver. Before he could do so, the war ended. He spent the next six months as a timekeeper at the Anaconda Copper Mining Company plant in Great Falls marking time until he received further orders. It gave him an insight into another side of the "real world"— one with which, he later wrote, "...I was not much impressed."

In October 1953, Ian was ordered to report to an Air Force office at Solana Beach, California, 20 miles north of San Diego. In a letter written to his Uncle Harry, he says, "It was fantastic duty. Our duties were to audit defense contractors in the area who had military contracts. My bosses were CPA's. I learned a great deal and probably had more responsibility than I should have had at my age. However, it was apparent to me that I didn't want to be an accountant for the rest of my life...."

"All in all," he concludes, "my Air Force experience was very beneficial. It taught me more about basic accounting procedures than I had learned at the University of Montana."

In October 1955, Ian was discharged early from the Air Force to enter graduate school at the University of California at Berkeley. " I was

The original thesis that Ian created for his MBA degree in 1956.

able to use the G.I. Bill to defray my expenses at Cal," he adds, in typical Scottish fashion.

It was while Ian Davidson was in graduate school that the idea for modern-day DADCO was born. His master's thesis, required for an M.B.A. degree, outlined the steps to be taken and procedures to be followed to develop and grow a successful securities organization in a predominately rural area like his native Montana. His father's firm provided the model for his case study. It is early evidence that he was already headed in the direction his career would take. It is also the basic blueprint for the development of the DADCO companies in the years since.

The truly remarkable fact about the Davidson thesis is that it has never lost its relevance to the present, even though it was developed to meet conditions existing nearly a half century ago. Ian's thesis was completed in 1956. Dwight Eisenhower was president. Still ahead was the Vietnam War and the social revolution it spawned. The Dow Jones

Industrial Average had not yet reached 500. The computer existed only in science-fiction imagination. So did the idea of space travel, nuclear energy, e-mail, and the fax machine.

In 1956, 1700 of the then 3,000 members of the National Association of Securities Dealers (NASD) employed five or fewer people. In 1998, more than 5,500 NASD member firms employed over 500,000 people—with the 700 largest firms doing 98% of the business. The growth of the securities industry has exploded over the past 40 years, and the competitive environment in which DADCO has grown has been intense. DADCO was the 90th largest firm based upon capital in 1999. Yet the basic criteria for success set forth by Ian in his paper in 1956 are the same criteria which are essential for success today. Times, customs and social mores have changed. New ways of fulfilling human needs and wants have been discovered and refined. But human nature remains largely unchanged, and human desires for life's necessities and niceties are virtually the same as they were at the dawn of history.

Any successful business must produce a product or a service which satisfies some human need. It must also have access to enough potential users for the product or service to justify the cost of supplying them. In economic terms it is called measuring the market potential. Factors like population, wealth, capacity for growth, and how adequately a particular market is presently served all play a part in such measurement.

To be successful, a business must deliver the product or service it promises at a price the customer can afford to pay. If more than one person is involved, the role of each must be identified, and the ability of each to fill the role must be assessed. In short, what jobs need to be filled, how many people will be needed, and can they do the job?

Ian's thesis established that it was necessary for a small firm to successfully establish itself as a leader in some particular niche of the market if it was to grow and prosper. In his study of Gibson Associates, Ian identified its niche as a firm which could provide superior service at a competitive price through personal service. It was the dominant goal in the early development of the firm, and remains so today.

In 1956, Ian Davidson stressed the necessity to measure the market potential as a prelude to any change in its operating procedures. Then, it involved only one two-person office; today, multiple offices employing hundreds of people in seven states. Yet the market potential, both internally and externally, is still carefully measured by every DADCO company before any expansion is considered.

Efficient and effective operating procedures are still the subject of constant and intensive scrutiny to be sure that DADCO customers receive the best service possible for the price they pay—just as the Davidson thesis recommended.

A major section of the thesis concerned itself with the value of stock exchange membership to the development of Gibson Associates. For a regional firm, a regional exchange was recommended. For the past twelve years, a DADCO officer has served on the Board of Governors of the Pacific Exchange; Ian Davidson has served as its highest non-administrative officer; and DADCO now operates its largest specialist post operation.

Stock exchange membership played an important role in turning around the fortunes of Gibson Associates. In the ensuing years, it has helped to push DADCO to the forefront as the premier investment firm in its region.

At first glance, it may seem to be an exercise in self-aggrandizement to equate Ian Davidson's Berkeley thesis with the Magna Charta and the U.S. Constitution in historic significance. Yet, the basic principles which it developed to guide the growth of the DADCO companies have resulted in financial freedom for thousands of citizens in the modest confines of the Northern Rocky Mountain and Pacific Coast region in much the same manner as did the Magna Charta and Constitution to assure political and human freedom for millions in a much larger arena.

Sometimes great oaks truly do grow from little acorns.

Clearing the Deck

Oliver Wendell Holmes, the noted jurist, is credited with the aphorism that "a great institution is but the lengthened shadow of a great individual." History is replete with examples.

Who can separate the automobile industry from Henry Ford or Walter Chrysler?—or the telephone from Alexander Graham Bell?—or electronics from Thomas Alva Edison? The Mayo brothers are still the epitome of modern group medicine; while, when we think of computers, Bill Gates and Steven Jobs immediately come to mind. In sports, Babe Ruth and Ty Cobb still symbolize the best in baseball; Knute Rockne and Vince Lombardi in football; while Arnold Palmer and Jack Nicklaus still set the standard in professional golf for the likes of Tiger Woods to emulate.

It may seem presumptuous to suggest that Ian Davidson has set a new standard for the entire financial services industry, but it is certainly no exaggeration to say that today's DADCO is an increasingly-lengthening extension of Ian Davidson, its chief architect. In 1985, Western Business magazine selected Ian as its Business Executive of the year. In an article covering the event, Bruce Madsen, recently retired vice chairman of DADCO, flatly stated that "Ian Davidson is D.A. Davidson & Co." This has not changed since. Also, more and more, the company he heads is becoming recognized in its field as one leading a whole industry to new heights of acceptance and respect through its example.

All this, however, was but a hope and a promise for the future when Ian first arrived on the job in February, 1958. Several more urgent immediate problems clamored for attention—questions like: where is the money coming from to pay him? The firm had grossed a mere $17,500 in total income the previous year. This had to cover wages for

Ralph Allison with Ian Davidson in 1987—more than 50 years after he was hired by D.A. Davidson as his first employee.

Mr. Davidson and a secretary, as well as rent, utilities, wire charges and other operating costs required to stay in business. Yet, there they were, taking on a new employee who expected to be paid. "I'm not sure [my Dad] was very excited when I showed up," Ian commented in a recent newspaper interview about his decision to join his father in 1958.

When D.A. Davidson opened his office in 1935, it was a branch of E.J. Gibson, Inc., with headquarters in Butte. It was Gibson's only branch. Davidson was a minority shareholder. The initial staff was composed of Mr. Davidson, Ann Weldele, a secretary/cashier who ran the clerical operations with an iron hand, and Ralph Allison, a young man on his first job, who posted stock quotations on a chalkboard in the reception area. Quotations were received by earphone from a wire operator at E.A. Pierce & Co. (later to become a part of what is now the Merrill Lynch organization). They were relayed by an open communications wire through Western Union. Allison left the firm after four years, leaving Dave Davidson and Ann Weldele as its sole employees until Ian joined it 18 years later. In the interim, it was Dave Davidson himself who posted the quotations.

In 1941, the Davidson family purchased the Gibson stock and renamed the firm Gibson Associates. David A. Davidson was president, with his brothers, Harry and Charles, as directors.

When Ian Davidson came aboard in 1958, the Dow Jones Industrial Average stood at 466.62. The firm's net worth was $33,000 and had grossed $17,500 in net income in the previous year. The economy had enjoyed a period of modest growth and prosperity after recovery from the Great Depression and World War II. But it was about to enter into the decade of the turbulent sixties with its great social and technological revolution. It was to be a period fraught with peril and trauma; but one which promised great rewards for those who could manage change while holding fast to those enduring principles on which America's free market system and democratic freedoms had been built.

Ian's first priority was to build a "book" of personal customers as quickly as possible so that the commissions he generated would at least cover his personal wages. Fortunately, it was a part of the business which he enjoyed. It channeled his love of people inherited from his mother into a direct relationship with his customers. He could follow firsthand the results of his advice. He has always made time to work his personal customer accounts. It has been one of the trademarks of his success. They are given a top priority on his schedule. One of his chief regrets is that, as the firm has grown, he has had less and less time to devote to this activity. In recent years, he has had to turn many of his old customers over to others to assure that they receive adequate follow-up service.

Getting new customers, however, was only one side of the equation. It was also necessary to reduce the costs of executing orders for the purchase or sale of stocks and bonds. Otherwise, the firm could not remain competitive with its competition. It was one of the major obstacles to the long-term success of the Gibson firm that Ian had pinpointed in his thesis.

When Ian joined the firm, it was a member of the Chicago Board of Trade (CBOT). Membership was required for any dealer who bought or sold contracts in such commodities as wheat, corn, gold, silver, pork bellies, etc. Commodity trading was—and still is—a very volatile market and never did fit well with the conservative Davidson character. In 1974, the firm voluntarily terminated its involvement with these markets, sold its CBOT membership, and has not traded in commodities since.

In 1958, commodity orders constituted only about 10% of Gibson's production. The vast majority of its business came from the purchase or sale of stocks and bonds; yet the firm was not a member of any securities exchange. Removing this obstacle to growth was one of the first actions taken by Ian Davidson when he joined the firm in 1958. He selected the recently formed Pacific Coast Stock Exchange. It was consistent with a recommendation in his MBA thesis. It was the first step in what has been a long and profitable association of D.A. Davidson & Co. with the Pacific Exchange.

For those not familiar with the way stocks and bonds are bought or sold, a step back might be useful. It will allow them to better understand the handicap under which Dave Davidson labored in his early years in the business.

At that time, shares of stock in any publicly traded corporation were bought or sold only through an exchange recognized by, and subject to, the rules and regulations of the Securities Act of 1934. Any firm or individual who wishes to trade (buy or sell) stocks must be registered with the NASD. In 1935 the law allowed a member of an exchange to add a fixed commission, set by the exchanges and approved by the SEC, to the price of a stock to cover its cost of executing orders, transferring the ownership of the shares, collecting and distributing dividend payments, selling expenses and the like.

(In 1975, fixed commissions were eliminated by SEC mandate. Each dealer is now allowed to set its own charges.)

Prior to the time that Ian joined it in 1958, Gibson Associates was not a member of a stock exchange. It executed its orders through a correspondent's agreement with J.A. Hogle Co. in Salt Lake City. Hogle received the fixed commission allowed it as an exchange member. The only way Gibson could cover its costs and make a profit was to charge the customer an additional fee. This put Gibson at a serious competitive disadvantage. It had to ask customers to pay more for the same share of stock than they could go down the street and buy it from a competitor. Because friendship and goodwill extend only so far, the override commission was kept as low as possible. Gibson's profit was very small and, in order to be able to make enough to survive as a business, it had to make up in added volume what it would have normally received from the fixed commission paid to Hogle. This arrangement allowed Gibson to be moderately profitable until 1947 when Piper Jaffray opened an office in Great Falls. From then until it became a member of the Pacific Stock Exchange in 1958, it suffered a small loss each year. It simply could not compete with a New York Exchange member without being a member of a competitive regional exchange.

Ian's thesis was emphatic that exchange membership was essential if

Gibson Associates was to survive and grow. At the time, there were six major stock exchanges in the country. The New York Stock Exchange (NYSE) was the largest, the most prestigious, and the most expensive. It dealt only with those companies which did a large national or multi-national business.

The American, also based in New York, was the second largest stock exchange. In its early days, it was known as the Curb Exchange. Tradition has it that its early stock transactions were completed on the sidewalk outside the NYSE—hence, the nickname. The American Exchange deals primarily with the stock offerings of smaller, lesser known companies whose shares are less-widely traded than those on the NYSE.

The New York and the American Stock Exchanges were known as national exchanges. The Midwest Stock Exchange in Chicago, the Los Angeles Stock Exchange, and the San Francisco Stock Exchange, among others, were classified as regional exchanges. For those firms whose operations were limited to a particular geographical location or to a particular segment of the market, a regional exchange offered a satisfactory alternative to a national exchange at a fraction of the cost of membership and with much less stringent membership requirements.

In 1956 Ian's study recommended the Midwest (now the Chicago Stock Exchange) as the choice for Gibson Associates. However, by the time the firm was ready to apply for membership in 1958, the Los Angeles and San Francisco Stock Exchanges had merged to form the Pacific Coast Stock Exchange (PSE) with a separate trading floor in each community. Unlike other exchanges, it accepted corporations as members. It also required as little as $25,000 in capital to qualify. So it was the Pacific Coast Stock Exchange—Los Angeles Division which was selected. In 1970, it also purchased a membership in the Midwest (now Chicago) Exchange.

The Pacific selection proved to be a great fit for both the firm and the Exchange. The PSE has become a major exchange, particularly involving issues by multi-national and international corporations. In 1958, the firm paid $2,825 for its first membership; in 1999 a seat sells for between $450,000 and $500,000. D.A. Davidson & Co. maintains fifteen specialist posts—ten in San Francisco and five in Los Angeles. By the start of the new millennium, they will handle a combined annual trading volume well in excess of 1.2 billion shares. It is the largest specialist operations on the PSE; and the performance of all of its fifteen posts have consistently been ranked among the top PSE specialist posts based on an ongoing quarterly evaluation of customer satisfaction conducted by the Exchange.

From 1987 to 1996, Ian Davidson served as a member of the Board of Governors of what, through a series of name changes, is now the Pacific Exchange, and in 1992 was Vice Chairman of the Exchange, its highest non-administrative position. When elected a PSE Governor in 1987, he was the first Montanan ever to serve on the governing board of any major exchange. In 1996, Bruce Madsen, Vice Chairman of DADCO, was elected to fill the vacancy created by Ian's retirement from the Board. Dave Hultman, Vice President in charge of all DAD PSE Specialist activities, also serves on the Board and, in 1999, has been elected to serve as its Vice Chairman. The long association of D.A. Davidson & Co. with the PSE continues without interruption.

With a growing number of new customers and an exchange membership which allowed it to receive a competitive commission on its business, Gibson's revenue picture was much brighter at the end of 1958 than at its beginning. Ian and his brother, Dave, had joined their uncles as directors, and Ian had been named a company officer. Its new membership on the Pacific Coast Stock Exchange gave it access to other major stock exchanges. This expanded the number of issues it could offer its customers at prices fully competitive with any of its competitors. But there was one major piece of unfinished business still remaining before it embarked on its quest to become a major power in its niche.

In the high-flying 1920s, a firm headed by H.B. Lake was the sole securities dealer in Great Falls. In the aftermath of the 1929 stock market crash, Lake's firm went bankrupt under highly questionable circumstances. Rumors of fraud and stock manipulation were rampant in the community. It left many investors with battered bank accounts and a bitter taste about anything associated with stock investing. It was in this climate that Dave Davidson opened the E.J. Gibson office in 1935.

There was no connection between H.B. Lake and E.J. Gibson. But the Lake debacle made the entire securities industry almost a dirty word in the minds of many. When E.J. Gibson opened a Great Falls office in 1935, its image was stained by a common suspicion that its business was not entirely honorable. It was also widely assumed that Lake and Gibson were somehow connected. While not true, the misperception was another obstacle for Dave Davidson to overcome. Even a change of name to Gibson Associates, and the purchase of the entire ownership by the Davidson family in 1941 was not sufficient to entirely erase the bitterness caused by the Lake scandal.

None of it had touched Dave Davidson personally. However, in February 1959, to eliminate any stigma which might still be attached to the name, and more important, to honor and pay tribute to the vision, the courage, and the steadfastness of David Adams Davidson in the difficult years during and following the Great Depression, Gibson Associates was renamed D.A. Davidson & Co. (DAD). It honored the heritage of the Davidson family, and gave a new beginning to what was to become one of the industry's—and the nation's—outstanding success stories.

This accomplished, the newly-named firm did not dawdle. In 1956, Ian made this recommendation in his thesis: "On the basis of the income data, Helena may be a good location for a branch office of a firm offering complete investment service. Since Great Falls is the closest large city to Helena, it would be a convenient location for Gibson Associates to establish a branch office." In 1959, he adopted his own recommendation. On May 4th, D.A. Davidson & Co. opened its first branch office in Helena. The office was located in the prestigious Power Block with James E. Howeth (later to become Montana's first Commissioner of the Montana Board of Investments) as its sole broker-manager. With a secretary in the Helena office, it brought the firm's total work force to five—three in Great Falls and two in Helena.

The foundation had been firmly laid, the deck had been cleared, and Ian Davidson was on his way.

Passing the Torch

As is frequently the case when an unusual individual becomes a part of an existing enterprise and takes it to new heights, the story of DADCO is a story in two parts: that part which took place before his arrival and that which happened after. Were I a theologian recounting the history of the Judeo-Christian religion, I could cite the Holy Bible with its Old and New Testaments, as an example. The first was the story of a people in desperate search of an identity; the second of a people who found it in the person of a great leader.

So it was with DADCO. The story of its early years is a story of survival as a viable concern. It was born in the economic chaos of deep depression. It was nurtured and grew to adolescence during the frantic confusion of the World War II years. The country was groping to reconcile its traditional way of life with that of a leader of democracy in a world awash in communism and other foreign ideologies. Though a period of relative prosperity returned to the country in the early years after the war, a pervasive feeling of unease and unrest overlay a society generally satisfied with its lot. Increasingly, political solutions dominated economic and social problems. Concern about the spread of communism occupied more and more of the attention of national leaders. Hot spots in Korea and Southeast Asia heated up. Our position as a world leader required that the United States become actively involved, first in an advisory capacity; then as an active participant; and finally, as virtually the sole opponent of the spread of communism in the free world.

Such was the situation when Ian B. Davidson joined Gibson Associates in February 1959 to help his father move it to a place of prominence in its industry. He brought to it a knowledge and understanding, not only of the securities business, but also of the people in his area—those he would hire, and those who would become his customers. He would become the single most dominant force in transforming a two-person local stock brokerage office into a multi-office, multi-state financial services power in a seven-state region in which it has chosen to restrict its activities. In the doing, he faced business triumph and tragedy in a society in the throes of a social revolution as chaotic, in its own way, as had been depression and war in his father's day.

The first part of our story concerned the struggles of David Adams Davidson; the second is an account of the impressive superstructure erected by Ian Bruce Davidson on the foundation laid by his father.

The years of Gibson Associates and its predecessor were marked by depression, war, and a tenuous start toward economic recovery. The major mission of David A. Davidson during those years was to keep his business afloat and viable. He had no great burning desire to expand beyond the comfortable confines of his hometown area. His innate Scottish conservatism rebelled at even the modest suggestion recommended in Ian's study of his firm that it seek membership in a regional stock exchange. It would require an investment of money which, in his view, his company simply could not afford to make.

But times were changing, both in the country and in the community. A bunch of visionary "whiz kids" in Silicon Valley in California and other places were already beginning to talk seriously about machines which would make those of the fictional Buck Rogers commonplace. Words like "chips" and "bytes" and "semiconductors" and "downloading" were increasingly creeping into the lexicon of business. Financial products like stocks, bonds, mortgages, real estate, insurance, and bank accounts were no longer regarded as separate avenues to financial well-being, in deadly competition with each other, but as different rooms in the same structure, each to be used for a specific purpose in a well-constructed house of financial security. Social Security, first enacted as an old age retirement plan the year D.A. Davidson opened his office in the Steele Building, had grown, with the addition of family death benefits and Medicaid-Medicare health care payments, to become, for most people, the foundation on which an individual would erect his or her own house of financial security.

Ian Davidson foresaw the potential possibilities for a firm like his father's, even if he did not yet fully comprehend their scope or the intricacy of the details which would be required to achieve them. He knew that to survive, it must make some drastic changes in its traditional way of doing business. The reluctance of the average citizen to entrust their savings to the stock market after the 1929 debacle had limited competition. But by the mid-to-late '50s, that was beginning to change. Unless it made some drastic changes in the way it had done business in the past, its future seemed doomed.

Even the competition sensed it.

In an interesting historical sidelight, in 1950, Mr. Piper, CEO of PJH, together with Ted Hodges, its local manager, offered David A. Davidson an opportunity to join PJH, and to either sell his firm to Piper, or to liquidate it. Dave responded that he was totally disinterested.

Dave's fierce independence and determination were laudable, but they in no way solved the very real problems facing Gibson Associates. The firm was in an untenable competitive position which could only get worse. It lacked the trained people to provide an ongoing level of service necessary to get and retain customers. To add to its woes, it was about to face the turmoil of the great social and ideological revolution of the 1960s.

It was in that period that three separate and distinct phenomena converged to challenge many of the fundamental social, moral, and ethical values on which our nation had been founded.

The first was a loss of confidence in the integrity and competence of our national leaders and the institutions they represented. It had its roots in the communist paranoia of the Senator Joseph McCarthy era. It was heightened by our country's ill-advised military misadventures in Southeast Asia. In the self-styled "police action" in Korea, American interests were so vague that the conflict was never elevated to the status of a full-blown war. A rift between General MacArthur and President Truman brought into focus a serious conflict between the military and civilian establishment as to the proper conduct of the war. The Korean venture ended in an uneasy truce which still exists today.

As the Far East military attention moved to Vietnam, and the body count mounted without any discernible resolution—(between the Korean and Vietnam conflicts, more than 112,000 young Americans lost their lives)—more and more people questioned the competency and commitment of both their military and their political leaders. Inflation started to wreak economic havoc at home, yet no one in authority seemed to be able to tell either the troops in the field or the folks back home why these boys were fighting and dying—or for what. It did not help that the Vietnam War was the first in which Americans could witness first hand from their living rooms every night the horrors of a war fought in a far-off land as it happened via transcontinental television. It was a graphic portrayal of what war was really like—and it was not pretty!

Protest marches, sit-ins, and emotionally-charged rallies on college campuses, in business establishments, and in the streets, erupted into full-scale revolt. Police and riot squads were called to restore order. Respect for law further eroded when protesting students were killed at a rally on the campus of Kent State University by inexperienced national guardsmen who panicked when unable to restore order. The political situation became so explosive that, while it did not drive President Johnson from office, it did deter him from seeking reelection.

The Vietnam disaster ended in full military capitulation. Troops were hastily withdrawn and returned home to face a climate of bitter recrimination against those who had answered their country's call to serve. America had suffered the first military defeat in its history—and the blame game started. The long finger pointed, not only in the direction of the military and political establishment, but also to educational, religious, business and other institutions which represented the established order. Their trustworthiness, and even their relevance to modern-day society, was called into serious question.

The final straw was a bungled Watergate burglary. It exposed a seamy side of partisan politics and of the presidency itself. It drove Richard Nixon from the Oval Office and shook the faith of even the staunchest patriots in the integrity of the leaders of their government institutions at all levels. Those shock waves still reverberate today.

The cynicism and disillusion arising from the exposure of the human foibles of time-honored institutions and their leaders was carried over into the personal values system of the so-called "baby boomers" just coming to maturity. It spawned a second phenomenon.

The atrocities of war were seen for the first time in history in all their horror through the power of television. The exposed ineptness of their political and military leaders, and the fury of the civil unrest it created, combined to shatter their faith in the validity of age-old values and institutions. Family, church, service clubs, and all institutions that taught the old-fashioned virtues of concern for neighbor, love of country, benevolence toward those less fortunate, love of God, and respect for sacred things became subjects of their doubt. Duty, accountability, responsibility, and marital fidelity became targets of the derision of avant-garde apostles who preached a doctrine that the chief purpose in life was self-gratification. Whatever makes you happy and enables you to feel good, ran their text, is ethically and morally acceptable. The "me" generation was born.

The educational establishment climbed aboard. No longer was the chief aim of public school to impart knowledge. Rather, it was to guard and nurture the self-esteem of the student. Better to give a failing student a passing grade than to risk shattering his self-esteem by requiring him to face the consequences of his failures. "Me" generation parents, eager to shed the shackles of parental responsibility, happily turned over to the school the responsibility for setting the boundaries of behavior for their children. Vigilant social workers and hungry trial lawyers made sure that the boundaries were broad enough to accommodate each new moral creed. It was justified under the guise of protecting the child from abuse or mistreatment. Many kids soon learned that they could get away with almost anything.

All this created a vacuum into which selfishness, greed, and concern only for one's well-being flowed. Tobacco, alcohol, and mood-altering drugs were glorified as self-esteem enhancers. Unrestrained sex became socially acceptable as a form of "feel-good" recreation. Any attempt at any restraint, however slight, immediately drew angry charges as an attack by blue-nosed religious fanatics on personal freedom.

While loss of trust in the country's leadership, and the resultant moral and ethical vacuum it created was taking place, a third phenomenon appeared on the scene in the form of militant feminism. For many years, women had occupied a second-class role in the economic and political life of society. Since Civil War days, periodic efforts by a few feminist pioneers had successfully gained for women the right to vote, to own property, and to hold public office. A few of the more daring attempted to compete with men in the business arena; but, except for such fields as teaching, nursing, and clerical support services, traditionally regarded as "women's work," it was not until World War II that Rosie the Riveter proved that women could also do "men's work." She declined to return peaceably to the kitchen when it was over. From that point on, more and more women set out to balance their time-honored role of homemaker and chief child-rearer with a career in such traditionally male-dominated bastions as law, accounting, medicine, business, and others. Even the military was not exempt. By the mid-1990s, well over half of all women of working age were gainfully employed outside the home.

These phenomena gave rise to a whole host of social problems. The loss of public confidence in the integrity and competence of their government and its leaders, the revolt of the "me" generation against conventional society, and the emergence of feminism all combined to create social and moral confusion. Youth no longer had strictly defined boundaries of behavior within which to fashion their values. They suddenly found themselves with unrestrained freedom and few guidelines as to how to handle it. The elderly saw old familiar values come under fire with no safe haven to which they could turn. The Baby Boom generation, reveling in its new-found freedom from social and moral restraints, wasted no time taking full advantage of them. The result was a society which glorified self-gratification and whose mantra was "anything goes!"

Yet society suddenly seemed surprised and appalled when divorce rates exploded, AIDS became a national epidemic, the number of single-parent families soared, SAT scores plummeted, teenage pregnancies and juvenile crime shot off the charts, and dead-beat fathers became a national scandal.

Newton's Law—for every action there is an opposite and equal reaction—had not been repealed.

It was in this era of social turmoil that Ian Davidson set out to build a business superstructure on the foundation which his father had carefully laid during years of severe economic trauma. Just as David A. Davidson had gambled that old-fashioned honesty, industry and fair-dealing would overcome the distrust and suspicion rampant after the 1929 collapse, Ian had faith that the same virtues, when challenged in the 1960s by a generation intoxicated by rebellion and disenchanted by the ineptness and ethical and moral confusion displayed by so many of its institutions, would still prevail. He opted to hire the best people he could find who would buy into what has become the DADCO culture of putting the customer first in all their dealings. He made them partners in the venture, sharing ownership and profits with them and rewarding them as the firm prospered. He saw to it that they were trained well for the work they were asked to do, and had the tools and technical support needed to do it. He encouraged their participation in the affairs of the communities in which they lived; and took the lead by accepting leadership positions in the community and the industry. He provided financial support as well, through family and business gifts, for a variety of educational, cultural, and social institutions and causes.

This was not a portrait of the successful corporate executive of the times as painted by press, politician, and the radical apostles of the "good life." That picture was one of a high-living, self-centered, hard-charging individual, interested only in leveraging company assets to inflate the price of its stock so he could move higher on the list of the Forbes' richest.

Ian Davidson is a self-described contrarian. His greatest reward is the respect and commendation of his colleagues, customers, competitors, and fellow citizens. His greatest satisfaction lies in the part he has played in erecting permanent memorials to the years he has spent on the stage of life: the business he has built—the Honors College which bears his name—the museums he assisted, both with donations and financial expertise— and the gratitude of thousands of customers who have realized dreams and become financially secure because of his stewardship and that of the colleagues with whom he has surrounded himself.

Ian B. Davidson

In 1958, he set out to steer his father's business on a course which had as its primary goal to improve the life of its customers, and the communities in which they lived. The final test was how well its customers prospered. In the doing, he, and those associated with him, have prospered beyond their wildest expectations. Therein lies a message for all who would sacrifice quality for expediency or immediate gain. Old-fashioned values and virtues enabled Dave Davidson to succeed in a climate of economic fear and uncertainty. They enabled the business

Davidson Honors College at the University of Montana.

he established to grow, prosper, and become a leader among its peers under Ian in the turmoil of the '60s. It tells all who will listen that old values are still capable of producing great rewards for all who are willing to embrace them without reservation or compromise.

So we take leave of the Old Testament part of our narrative and move to the New. Until now we have largely recited past history—much of which took place before the majority of our potential readers were born. They have known about World War I, the euphoria of the '20s, and the Great Depression only by hearsay from the history books or from tales by old-timers like me. In an age of skepticism, we often find it hard to separate fact from faulty memory. For many, even the events of World War II, with its awful price in lives destroyed and a world turned topsy-turvy, are kept alive only by such poignant accounts as those found in Tom Brokaw's recent masterpiece, The Greatest Generation. Soon, Vietnam and its concomitant social revolution will join their ranks.

That is the reason we spent what, to some, may seem an undue amount of time on our recollections of this era which, among other notable events, saw the start and early development of the predecessor of the DADCO companies. We felt that it was important to try to give our readers a sense of the times in which the gestation of the enterprise occurred and the challenges it had to overcome. It may help them to better understand the importance of the DADCO culture which, in many ways, ran—and still runs—counter to that which prevails in today's society. It gives DADCO a uniqueness which sets it apart from many of its contemporaries.

What follows will probably be more familiar to many of you. Some may even have been a part of it in some measure. You'll learn what was done—and why—as we follow the unfolding of modern DADCO from one tiny three-person retail stock brokerage office in Great Falls, Montana to a financial mini-conglomerate with upwards of 30 offices in seven states employing well in excess of 700 people and offering a wide range of diversified financial and allied services to more than 100,000 customers, mainly concentrated in the Pacific Northwest. You'll meet some of the major contributors to its success, some of whom you may know personally or from a business relationship. We want you to be aware of the part they played in making DADCO the outstanding success it has been.

We hope you enjoy reading our account as much as we have enjoyed telling it.

PART II

Building a Home Base

The social revolt of the 1960s touched every segment of society, including newly-named D.A. Davidson & Co. Ian Davidson recognized this. He was perceptive enough to realize that his new firm, too, would have to do business differently in the future if it hoped to achieve the stature of pre-eminence he aspired for it. While Dave Davidson was still nominally in charge, more and more of the decision-making responsibility fell upon Ian. His energy, vision and personal contacts increasingly influenced company actions. It was he who convinced his father to look beyond the confines of their three-person office in Great Falls. He engineered the opening of the first branch office in Helena and hired Jim Howeth, an experienced securities analyst, to run it. He also made friends in Great Falls with Bill Macfadden, a young stockbroker from Minneapolis who had been sent to the Great Falls office of Piper, Jaffray and Hopwood (PJH) for training. Bill's father was a partner in PJH, and his plan was to allow Bill to gain field experience with the hope that he would return ready to move into an executive position in its Minneapolis headquarters. However, he failed to take the Montana lifestyle into account.

Bill Macfadden is a man with exceptionally strong ethical values. Prior to moving to Montana, he had spent time in its forests, working in logging camps as a young man. Though a Midwesterner by birth and educated in New England at Dartmouth College, he was impressed by Montana's lack of pretense and the openness of its people. Long before his move to Great Falls, he had resolved that, sooner or later, he wanted to live in Montana. The Great Falls opportunity was like an answer to a long-held dream. Ian and Bill became business friends. Joan-Nell had been a social friend of Nancy Davidson before their respective marriages.

Bill Mcfadden

Bill was deeply involved in the business, social and recreational life of Great Falls and was attracted by the trusting and friendly style of a small office. So, when the time came to return to the Midwest metropolis, Bill politely said, "No thanks," and became the third broker in D.A. Davidson's Great Falls branch office.

PJH's loss was DAD's gain. Bill Macfadden retired in 1990, after almost thirty years during which he served, among other things, as Executive Vice President of DAD and President of Financial Aims Corporation, one of the DADCO companies. During his tenure with FAC, assets under his management increased more than 15-fold. He also racked up an impressive record of community service, including a stint as president of the C.M. Russell Museum, a school board trustee, president of the hospital board, and a host of other community leadership posts.

Both he and Joan-Nell have continued to carry their commitment to their community into retirement: he with his work with people with disabilities through the Eagle Mount organization, and she in the field of mental health. Both have been widely recognized for their work in their respective fields of community work.

With the addition of Bill Macfadden, the Great Falls office in the Steele Building was getting crowded. It moved across the street to space in what was then the Great Falls National Bank. (The bank is now a part of the Wells Fargo-Norwest banking chain.) Shortly thereafter, Johan Miller replaced Ann Weldele as the firm's secretary/treasurer and immediately started training to become registered as DAD's first homegrown Account Executive. Johan came to DAD from the Great Falls National Bank where he had been a junior officer. In addition to studying for his registration, he also set about to revamp and reorganize all the firm's accounting procedures which, according to Johan, were the unique invention of Ms. Weldele. "They were a mess," he said bluntly. Johan was also among a group who had shared a house with Ian before his marriage, and is DADCO's second oldest employee still active with the firm. Very conservative in his investment philosophy, Johan Miller has achieved a widespread reputation for the manner in which he

Johan Miller at DAD's 50th Anniversary dinner.

serves his personal clients, whose loyalty to him is legendary.

Changes at DAD did not come easy. Visiting with Johan about some of those early days, he recalls, with a mixture of amusement and nostalgia, the clash of conflicting convictions between Ian and his father. Dave was of the old school. He remembered well the Depression years. He was steeped in Scottish conservatism that regarded debt and investing in an unknown future as the height of financial recklessness.

Ian, on the other hand, was convinced that ways of doing business, which may have been successful in the past, were no longer sure-fire guarantees for the future. Times and methods were changing; to compete, businesses must keep in step.

Dave, while conceding much of what Ian advocated, was still reluctant to undertake the required changes. He was on the downhill side of his career and was content, if not fully satisfied, with things as they were. Ian had the "fire in the belly" to become a much bigger frog in a much bigger puddle. His research for his thesis convinced him that he could do it.

The resulting arguments, sometimes heated, "made for some interesting times in the office," recalled Johan as he reminisced about his early days at DAD.

These first tentative steps might seem quite modest when measured against today's expansion pace, but at that time they were gigantic; particularly given the conservative Davidson nature and size of the investment required for even so modest an effort. But it was not long before the soundness of Ian's leadership began to pay off. By the time DAD opened its third office in Missoula in 1965, its total force numbered 31 people, and the net worth reached $165,000.

D.A. Davidson & Co. was beginning to attract attention as a player to be reckoned with in the brokerage business in Montana.

It had also outgrown its space in the Great Falls National Bank. It needed more room to grow. The downtown business district of Great Falls was reeling from the flight of many of its retail shops to a newly-constructed outlying shopping mall. It needed a shot in the arm to rekindle its viability. In October 1965 the opportunity arose to do both.

The one-story Steele Building in which Gibson Associates first started business was located in the heart of the Great Falls business district. The area had developed into a major financial center. The city's three largest banks and two of its three stock brokerage offices were located within a shade over one square block from each other. The largest bank had just announced plans to replace its existing building with a new one on the same site. The Steele Building was across the avenue. It was ideally located for another growing financial firm. It was also for sale.

The Steele Building was more than just a desirable business location. It was a site with considerable historical significance in the early development of Great Falls. During the '20s and '30s, it housed one of the city's most prominent "hangouts" for teens and grownups alike. Emerging local literary greats like Joseph Kinsey Howard, Norman Fox, Bob McCaig, Dan Cushman, and A.B. Guthrie had found support, encouragement, and research assistance at the bookstore of former high school English teacher, Gladys Williams, on the building's ground floor. Fritz Norby, one of the city's most popular early mayors, had his real estate office there. Most of the building's tenants had been, and many of their descendants still are, prominent in the growth of the city which, at the time, was Montana's largest.

It made little economic sense for D.A. Davidson & Co. to own its own building; but it appeared to offer an excellent investment opportunity for Ian Davidson to personally own it and rent space to DAD. He was just getting started in business, and his personal balance sheet did not justify a loan of the magnitude needed. However, he did own a sizable equity interest in a growing business, had already demonstrated his ability to manage it well, had the backing of some influential friends, and most important, had established an impeccable reputation for honesty and integrity.

These are the assets he took to his friend, the late Forrest Hedger, then president of the Great Falls National Bank. Both were enthusiastic about the proposed project. They also shared the same keen desire to improve and upgrade the downtown business environment. At the time, the Great Falls National Bank was a locally-owned institution, able to approve local loans at a local level. Hedger believed that the character of his customers was equal in importance to their financial assets when it came to loaning the bank's money. Ian met the test. The loan was approved, the purchase consummated, and in mid-July 1966 DAD returned to greatly-expanded ground-level space in the Steele Building, now owned by Ian Davidson. DAD was back where it had started 31 years earlier.

In the summer of 1968, opportunity again came knocking. Ian answered the call and triggered a series of events which would establish him as one of the rising stars in the Great Falls business community. Here's how Ian remembers it:

"One of the positives that had made the Steele Building loan attractive was that the building had been so solidly built that its foundation would support at least four additional stories. Forrest Hedger remembered this when an officer of a major insurance company called on him to see if he knew where his company might lease 10,000 square feet of prime office space for a planned expansion in Great Falls. He had been unable to find this much suitable space in any existing facility. Hedger referred the insurance officer to Ian Davidson.

"Following my discussion with Guy Brannon of Travelers Insurance," recalled Ian, "I asked my brother to prepare a rendering of what four additional stories on top of the Steele Building would look like. Ironically, the rendering turned out to be almost identical to the building he later designed.

"With this rendering—and a little luck—we were able to get a letter of commitment from Travelers Insurance Company to lease approximately 10,000 square feet at a rate of $5.20 per square foot. In 1968, this was a higher price than any other in Great Falls of which I was aware. Then came the struggle to get financing.

"After several meetings with local bankers, led by Forrest Hedger of Great Falls National, with participation by Adrian McLellan of First National and Jay McLeod of Bank of Montana Systems, I convinced them that this was a good loan. But it was not until my

The Davidson Building when it was first opened in 1969. D.A. Davidson & Co. occupied less than one-fourth of the space on the first floor.

A recent picture of the Davidson Building with the Liberty Center on the right. DADCO and its subsidiaries occupy about two-thirds of the space in the two buildings.

friend, Shawn Corette, a Butte attorney, got the First National Bank in Butte to agree to participate that Forrest Hedger was able to convince the group that it was worthwhile to take the risk, despite the fact that except for the fifth floor and a part of the fourth floor, the proposed addition had no other signed leases.

"Bids came in right at $1 million. Because the boiler in the existing structure could handle the additional space, elevator shafts formed in 1920 were already in place, and a concrete floor under a built-up roof provided a floor for a potential second story, the bid worked out to be an amazing $18 per square foot for building cost. Construction began in February 1969 and, unbelievably, was completed in November 1969. Travelers immediately moved in, adding nearly 100 new employees to the downtown work force."

The building was renamed the Davidson Building and took its place as one of the largest and most prestigious business addresses in downtown Great Falls.

At a reception honoring him upon his retirement from the bank, Forrest Hedger remarked that approving the Davidson loan was one of the best banking decisions he made in his long and illustrious banking career.

Fast-forwarding the building story into the present, DADCO now occupies about 80% of the original building, plus all of the lower level. The remaining space houses firms who are long-time lessees, most of whom have close business ties to DADCO. The building was full, yet the DADCO companies continued to grow.

The problem was rapidly reaching crisis proportion in 1996 when Ian Davidson got a second break. The first was when the Steele Building came to market at a time when D.A. Davidson & Co. first started to grow. The second came some 30 years later, when the Liberty Center directly across the street from the Davidson Building became available. Like the original Steele Building, it is an historic landmark. In its early days it housed the city's largest movie theatre. An unforgettable personal memory of my own youth was that of following the historic 1927 transatlantic flight of Charles A. Lindbergh to Paris in the Liberty Theatre via Pathé News and a loudspeaker. In 1982, the theatre was closed, the building sold, gutted, and transformed into a modern four-floor office and retail complex providing some 60,000 square feet of prime downtown office and retail space.

To meet DADCO's growing needs, a Davidson family real estate partnership, which now owns the Davidson Building, purchased the

Liberty Center. The purchase immediately doubled the firm's potential headquarter space. The city authorized the closure of the street to vehicular traffic between the two buildings so that it could be converted to a pedestrian plaza for public use. The two buildings have been connected by the first overhead skywalk built in Great Falls.

Some years earlier, anticipating a need for future expansion, the family partnership had purchased the remainder of the half block to the west of the Davidson Building. With the acquisition of the Liberty Center, the immediate need for more space has been satisfied, though the site is available for still further expansion if and when needed. In the meantime, Ian had a chance to realize another long-held dream: a downtown park area where the community can hold concerts and other outdoor events to add an ambience to the downtown business atmosphere. The area is now landscaped as an outdoor amphitheatre, paved for parking and protected by landscaped berms and trees, with space reserved to house an upscale restaurant facility.

It is a thank-you gift from the Davidson family to the city for its support of the firm.

To return to our original story:

In spite of all the activity arising from the construction of the Davidson Building in 1969, retail branch expansion continued. In 1965, just before Ian bought the Steele Building, DAD opened its third branch office in Missoula with Warren Drew as manager. One of the first brokers was Robert A. Braig. In 1969, Robert B. Bragg joined the office. Though spelled slightly different, their names were pronounced the same. This posed an interesting problem for those

Bob and Bev Braig

answering the phones in those early days. To compound the coincidence, both Bobs were born on the same day in the same year, and graduated in the same class at the University of Montana. They remained fast lifetime friends, though their careers took them on divergent paths—mostly, however, with DADCO. An enduring legend in company lore is that of their shared 40th birthday observance, masterminded by their wives, in a plot rivaling a John Grisham novel in its complexity.

Both will figure prominently as our story unfolds.

It was during this period that what we now call the DADCO Culture began to manifest itself. Warren Drew had come over from Great Falls as manager of the newly-opened Missoula Branch. The two Bobs, Braig and Bragg, joined him as brokers. Bev Braig recalls how the wives spent evenings and weekends painting walls, making curtains, and otherwise decorating the new quarters so that their husbands could concentrate their time and efforts getting new customers and taking care of old ones. "It developed a spirit of camaraderie," she reminisced, "that gave us a sense of belonging which made the work fun and forged a bond of family solidarity and lifetime friendships."

"It's something that a lot of the young kids and new people coming on don't seem to appreciate," Bev lamented. "They don't seem to realize that if you can spend your working life having fun doing worthwhile work that you enjoy with people you like and trust, the money will follow—not the other way around."

Thanks, Bev. It is one of the best definitions of the DADCO Culture we have heard.

While eager to expand DAD, Ian approached expansion with characteristic Davidson caution. While the first branch office outside Great Falls opened in Helena a year after Ian joined his father in 1958, it was six years before the next move into Missoula. A hallmark of Ian's management philosophy is to be sure each new unit in the organization is firmly established and paying its own way before moving on to the next.

In April 1968, D.A. Davidson & Co. opened its fourth Montana branch office in Butte with Charles W. Bowers as its manager. Charley Bowers is another of many legendary DAD "old-timers." He was a successful hardware merchant who first knew Ian Davidson as a customer. This contact left him so intrigued

Ian Davidson with Charley Bowers in 1966.

and enamored with the investment business that, when an opportunity came in 1965 to sell out his business, he switched careers and joined Ian's growing firm as a broker. Not only was he successful as a salesman, but the experience he had gained from running his own business had enabled him to develop valuable management skills. When the new branch was opened in Butte, Ian prevailed upon Charley to move to Butte to manage it. It was a challenging assignment.

Butte, Montana is a community which marches to a drumbeat all its own. In its glory days, it was a hell-roaring mining camp, yielding such vast riches in copper, zinc, cadmium, and other metals that it was known as the "richest hill on earth." All the vices and excesses familiarly associated with western mining camps flourished in Butte. But, in those early days, they were not only accepted and tolerated, but were raised to the status of civic assets. At one time, its wide-open "red light" district became a chief visitor attraction reminiscent, in miniature, of Amsterdam's famous bordello district.

By the time Charley Bowers moved to Butte, civilization had begun to temper its lifestyle and soften its image. But to this day it is a unique community, beloved and adored by its longtime residents as "Butte, America." However, for many who visit or who find themselves compelled to move there for whatever reason, a saying commonly-known in Montana as a "North Dakota joke" sums up their feelings: "The two most beautiful sights in Montana are Glacier National Park—and Butte in your rearview mirror!" Partly because of the haphazard way mining camps develop, Butte is not a town distinguished by its genteel tree-lined streets and stately missions. It still bears the scars of a ravaged environment. Its Berkeley Pit and surrounding area is best noted for being the largest single environmental superfund cleanup project in the entire country. But this has not been just a recent development. In reminiscing with Charley and Roberta Bowers about their move to Butte in 1968, she recalled a remark by a realtor when they were first looking for houses at the time of their move. After apologizing for the general lack of quality in the homes he had to show them, the realtor hastily assured them that "the people of Butte do not judge you by the house you live in. Their houses may not be the fanciest in the world, but these people still like to drive big cars and eat out often at family places."

The Bowers were never wholly comfortable living in Butte, but that didn't stop Charley from building a quality organization which was profitable almost from its start. Accompanying him on his move to Butte was Dave Wagner, also a broker in the Great Falls office. Dave is another pioneer DAD associate who deserves special mention. He played a key role in helping Charley get the new Butte office up and running. When Charley moved on to Billings in 1974, Dave took his place as Butte manager. In 1977 when DAD expanded into Bozeman, Dave Wagner was asked to head up the new office in the Gallatin Valley. He had been trained well by Charley Bowers, and the branch offices in both Butte and Bozeman continued to flourish under his leadership. Pat Connors took over as Butte manager when Dave left.

One of the most lasting legacies of Charley Bowers' stint in Butte was his recruitment of Pat Connors who, for nearly a quarter of a century, set the standard by which all D.A. Davidson brokers were judged. If Charley Bowers was an "outsider" in Butte, Pat Connors was the consummate "insider." Though just prior to joining DAD, he had been living in California, he was a personable Irishman who was born in Anaconda and knew the Butte-Anaconda area well. After finishing

Pat Connors

college at the University of Montana, he became a stockbroker in Sacramento, California with the since-defunct firm of Walston & Co. In the fall of 1968, on a vacation trip back to Butte, he had a chance meeting with Tim Connors (no relation to Pat) who was a broker in the recently established D.A. Davidson office in Butte. This led to a visit with Dave Wagner and Charley Bowers. "I was perfectly happy with my present situation," Pat recalled when we visited about his association with DAD, "but when you come from Butte, it is always home. Just before I left from my visit with Charley, I made an offhand remark about missing Butte." "If you ever want to come back," Charley said, "we'll find a desk for you."

"That was in November," Pat continued, "and after I got back to California, I started to think seriously about my brief visit at DAD. I was impressed with the organization, the people I had met, and their approach to the business. I also realized that I really did miss the Butte lifestyle. So, just before New Year's in 1969, I called Charley and told him I was taking him up on his offer—and threw him for a loop. The Butte office was not too big—and they had run out of desks! So I told Charley, 'That's alright; just get me a card table and a phone and put me in a back room somewhere!'"

That was 30 years ago—and for nearly 25 of those years Pat Connors has managed the Butte office while producing some $14 million in personal business—one of the great records in the entire securities industry.

In 1974, when DAD expanded into Billings, it again called on Charley Bowers' proven ability and expertise to establish a major branch office in what is now Montana's largest city. Charley again responded. When he retired in 1978, he had Phil Boggio on board and primed to step into his shoes. Though Phil has since relinquished the reins of management, he is still active as a Financial Consultant and a member of the Chairman's Council, DAD's top honor club.

The imprints left by Charley Bowers, Dave Wagner, and Pat Connors have been deep and lasting. Charley and Roberta still live, in retirement, in Billings; while Dave retired from DAD in 1981.

Two months after DAD opened its Butte branch, Ian Davidson was elected President of D.A. Davidson & Co. It had been ten years since he had joined forces with his father. In that time, the company had grown from three employees in one office and a net worth of $33,000 to 40 people in four offices and a net worth approaching $500,000. It had also expanded its services to include a new municipal bond department.

The shadow it was casting on the securities industry in Montana was growing longer and longer.

Growth begat added responsibility. As more and more people bought more and more stocks and bonds from DAD brokers, the pressure increased on the "back office" people to provide the kind of quality service that D.A. Davidson & Co. has always demanded. It is only when a trade takes place that service starts. When a person buys or sells a security, the price paid is set by the market as quoted on the exchange which handles the security. Once the transaction is completed, the ownership of the security must be transferred to its new owner, the proceeds, as well as any accrued dividends, must be collected and paid to the proper party, and the securities delivered to the new owner or put in safekeeping with the dealer.

To cover these costs, as well as selling expenses, research costs, clerical, computer, housing, administrative, and a seemingly endless stream of other expenses, each firm is allowed to add a transaction fee to the quoted price of the security. At one time, the amount allowed was fixed by the Securities and Exchange Commission and applied equally to all dealers. Now, the law allows each firm to set its own fee based on the extent of the service it provides for the customer. This has given rise to price discounting and creates a high degree of competition between the discount broker and the full-service investment firm.

In his MBA thesis, Ian emphasized the importance of building a unique niche for itself as a way for a small firm to establish itself in its region. At the time Ian came aboard, the firm was highly respected for its integrity and concern for its customers. Ian was convinced that if it continued to give superior service and grow value for those who did business with it, it would set DAD apart from its peers in the market in which it competed. To do this, he needed a back office second to none. Again another college acquaintance came to the rescue.

Stuart C. Nicholson was a University of Montana graduate with a degree in Accounting. Subsequently, he earned a CPA designation. Stu had about four years of accounting and auditing experience with two major forest product organizations prior to joining DAD in 1969. He was an internal auditor with Hoerner-Waldorf in St. Paul when Warren Drew, then an account executive with DAD, suggested Stu in response to Ian's request for suggestions for a person to fill the DAD position. Warren, subsequently the first manager of the Missoula branch, had been

Stu Nicholson

a classmate of Stu at U of M. Stu had been a student in a Finance Class which Ian taught at the U of M School of Business.

(Coincidentally, Delores Landsverk, one of Ian's long-time Administrative Assistants at DADCO, was in the same class. Another bit of "small world" trivia.)

Stu was ripe for Ian's offer to set up and run a back office operation for his growing securities firm. He had been born and raised in Missoula, and the traveling he had done in his recent jobs made him appreciate the quality of life found in the Big Sky Country. The culture of trust and personal concern for both customer and employee which he saw emerging at DAD was a sharp contrast to that which he had experienced in both of the firms with which he had been associated. "There was a lot of office politicking and jockeying for advantage," he recalled. "I wasn't sure I wanted to spend my life in that kind of environment. DAD gave me a chance to help build the kind of life I wanted to live."

Stu's duties and responsibilities have changed as the firm has grown.

No longer is he directly involved with the day-to-day concerns with the back office operations. He is now DADCO's Chief Financial Officer, with all of the responsibility which the title implies. He has served on the Board of Directors, the Executive Committee, and the Management Committee since each of these bodies was instituted, and has come to be regarded as the epitome of the DADCO culture. In 1998, he became the fourth recipient of the Bragg-Lewis-Knutson Community Service Award.

It would be hard to overstate the value of the contribution of Stu Nicholson to DADCO's success. In the securities business, the NASD closely monitors the transactions of each dealer to see that its orders are executed promptly and correctly. Any order entered in error is rejected until the error is corrected. In the 30 years since Stu Nicholson first set it up, this department has maintained one of the lowest rejection rates in the entire securities industry, despite a steady skyrocketing volume of orders. He has always been in the forefront in the use of technology. The company was among the leaders in the industry in its use; and each time a new system is installed, the Operations Department receives raves from both those installing the new system and the authorities regulating it, for the smoothness with which it was installed, and the lack of business disruption it caused.

Stu has also played a major role in attracting such people as Vinney Purpura, Darrell Block, and Keith Bjorsness to DADCO—not to mention his two sons, Doug and Tom. When he retires, Stu will leave a big hole to fill—but he will also leave a bevy of well-qualified successors prepared to guide the department he has so carefully built to its present state of excellence.

On October 16, 1970, David Adams Davidson died at the age of 76. He lived to see the firm he had created almost exactly 35 years earlier grow from a single two-person, hole-in-the wall office to branches in four of Montana's five largest cities. It boasted a spanking new home base, complete with a fledgling municipal bond department and a back office geared for growth. Ian, as its unquestioned leader, became Chairman, President and CEO. The net worth of the firm exceeded $850,000 and employed 67 people. DAD had become solidly established in the Montana business community and was poised to move into a much larger regional arena in the Pacific Northwest.

Carving a Niche

The dictionary defines a niche as a "suitable place or position." For our purpose, however, a niche is a segment of the securities business in which DADCO occupies a position of preeminence by reason of some advantage which is unique to its method of operation, or to the market it serves. Every business organization, of whatever size and nature has five constituencies to which it must answer. First are those who own the business. These may be as few as one or two in a "Mom-n-Pop" operation, or as many as millions in a multi-national corporate conglomerate. Owners are the ones who make final policy decisions, either directly or through designated representatives, about what the company does or does not do.

Then there are the employees—those who usually make only procedural decisions, if any, but who perform the tasks that enable the business to achieve its objectives. In very small businesses, owners and employees are often the same people; and many progressive firms are discovering that making employees owners in the enterprise is often a way to encourage greater productivity and business success.

The third constituency is the customer—those who buy and use the product or service which the business makes or provides. Of all the constituencies, the customer is by far the most important. Without someone to use or consume the product or service a company produces, the efforts of the best owners and the most productive employees are totally wasted and doomed to failure. Any business that ignores the best interests of the customer in favor of either of the other constituencies will ultimately find that all constituencies will suffer.

Fourth, the community which it serves and on which each unit depends for its success.

Finally, there is the larger society of which every business is a part. The impact of a very small business on society is usually quite small. If a four-person business lays off one of the four, its impact, while it is as devastating to the one laid off as it would be to the individual who is a part of a 1,000 person layoff, is barely felt by society. But the same 25% reduction in jobs in a force of 5,000 will cause serious repercussions throughout the entire community where it occurs. In like manner, if one-fourth of the entire national labor force loses their jobs, as they did during the Great Depression, its effect would rival that depression in its consequences.

As business organizations grow larger and larger, their decisions and actions increasingly affect the lives of their neighbors, their communities, and, to a degree, all segments of society.

The service or product a business offers—and the way it is produced—can either help people live together in harmony and personal satisfaction, or contribute to suspicion, distrust, and moral and ethical deterioration. The tobacco, gaming and some national resources industries (e.g., the spotted owl controversy in the forest products industry) are examples in which the health or welfare of some segment of society is perceived to run counter to the best interests of the business producing the product. All constituencies must be considered; but the most successful firms carve out a niche for themselves where they concentrate their major attention.

The Davidson thesis identified the small-town atmosphere in which people in Montana did business as a major asset of his father's struggling firm. The broker and the customer knew each other as individuals, not as faceless representatives of some distant financial entity. They could easily get together to discuss problems which might arise, or to explore new financial opportunities in an atmosphere of mutual trust. It was a business climate in which the Gibson firm excelled. David A. Davidson and the entire Davidson family were widely known and respected in the Great Falls community for their integrity and sincerity. They were respected for their financial knowledge and business judgment. In an industry just emerging from the devastating debacle of the Great Depression, and rife with suspicion about the stability and integrity of its financial institutions, this asset was of inestimable value. The reputation of the Gibson company was further enhanced by the fact that it was Montana's only domiciled securities firm. It was not only locally-managed and locally-owned, but was truly a homegrown business that the state could claim as one of its own.

As DADCO has grown and expanded throughout a seven-state region, it continues to focus on building the same kind of personal hometown relationships with its customers, its employees, and the communities in which it does business that served Dave Davidson so well in its early days. It is the foundation of what we know today as the DADCO culture.

The niche which DADCO aspires to occupy in the Northern Rocky Mountain/Pacific Northwest region in the financial services industry is to be the preeminent firm in its field. It has been its goal since Ian Davidson first joined his father in 1959. At first, it was but an unspoken vision, formalized in the firm's second mission statement in 1985. At that time it declared that the mission of DADCO is to deliver superior financial performance to meet the goals of its customers by "creating wealth and value for its clients, provide security and opportunities for its employees, and to enhance the environment in which both clients and employees lived and worked." In five reviews since that time, that mission has not changed. It has only been reaffirmed with more precise wording.

In Ian Davidson's thesis, he outlined the areas which he saw as necessary for Gibson Associates to address in order to survive and grow. Basically, they were the same areas contained in D.A. Davidson's first strategic plan formulated in 1982, and repeated in every revision since. They all emphasize that for a financial services business to excel in its field, it must be staffed with people with superior product knowledge who are thoroughly trained and constantly retrained in how to put their knowledge to work to meet the financial needs and wants of their clients. They must have access to the most modern and up-to-date tools available to assist them. They must know how to properly use those tools, and they must have the technical support to back them up when something goes awry. Above all, they must buy into and be fully committed to the firm's culture and its goal to be the best there is in their field.

That was the challenge to Gibson Associates in 1956. That is DADCO's challenge today.

The "people" part of a business starts with selection—choosing workers with the skills and attitudes to carry out that part of the firm's mission with which they are charged. One of the thorniest problems facing modern society is the apparent failure of so many to make the link between the lack of marketable skills and the inability to get and hold a job. Few organizations can survive, and none can excel, with a work force composed of people with mediocre skills. It is the one incontrovertible argument for the need to establish a level of skill and understanding which those who are graduated from our educational institutions must meet before they are presented to the workplace as possessing the basic ability necessary to function effectively in today's society. The fact that the subjects are hard, or the student's home environment is not conducive to learning, or that the background from which the student comes may be less than ideal, or that the skills of the teacher are mediocre, are irrelevant to the basic purpose for which people are educated. If a person cannot read and understands what he reads, or be able to communicate so that he can be understood, or make simple mathematical calculations and know what they mean, he is a functional illiterate without employable skills to offer an employer in exchange for the opportunity to earn a paycheck. It makes no difference *why*. It is only important that he does—or does not—have these skills. On that fact rests his future as a productive member of society.

Our nation's founding fathers recognized that fact when they established America's free and universal public school system. But in a day when protecting the self-esteem of the young seems to be more important than requiring them to become functionally literate before bestowing its certificate of competence on them, we have allowed political, social, racial and sectarian special interests to obscure the primary function of public education. By so doing, it has become a vehicle to advance social and political agendas, which severely hampers its ability to do its basic job of preparing a functionally literate work force to meet America's requirements.

DADCO's business is becoming increasingly more technical and more complex. It requires a work force with increasingly higher skill levels, and which has more and more knowledge about every facet of its business. If it is to be the premier player in its field, it must have a skilled and educated work force second to none. Continuing education enjoys a high priority in the DADCO strategic plan.

Careful selection has been a hallmark of DADCO's success from its modern beginnings in 1958. Most of its early employees were hand-picked by Ian Davidson who knew each personally. He knew they were his kind of people. As the firm has grown and its operations divided among multiple branches and departments which require, in many cases, a high degree of specialized technical competence, this kind of personal attention is no longer centered in one person. But its commitment to excellence in the quality of its work force has never wavered. It not only must have people with the technical skills required to provide the service to customers which each situation demands, but it also wants each to become a part of an integrated team, committed to DADCO values, and working together to realize its vision and accomplish its mission.

Once selected, each employee is given the opportunity to grow professionally. Not only is each trained by professional trainers for the specific requirements of the job, but each learns how his or her job relates to the overall success of the firm and its ability to grow value for the customer. The National Association of Securities Dealers requires those who provide financial advice or information to others to be qualified to do so. It demands that every Financial Consultant be registered by satisfactorily completing a comprehensive uniform examination. If they are new to DAD and not already registered, they must complete a 12-week training course and successfully pass the required NASD examinations. The training is offered by DAD at its corporate headquarters in a typical classroom setting under the direction of trained instructors. The firm pays the costs, including the salary of the trainee. These classes are also open to unregistered employees who wish to improve their skills and qualify for advancement.

They are also open to student interns under DADCO's College Intern Program. This program, started in 1985, provides students, usually seniors in regional universities who are interested in a career in some phase of the financial services industry, an opportunity to get an in-depth look at the industry before committing to a career. Interns are given the same training and must meet the same requirements as all others in the class. If they successfully pass the NASD examinations, they qualify for registration, pending any experience requirements involved. The firm pays for their housing, meals and other costs while they are in training. They receive college credit for their work.

DADCO has benefited in several ways from the Intern Program. The participating schools have been enthusiastic about the opportunities afforded its young people. The program has enhanced the reputation of the firm in the educational community as a quality company. It has also proven to be a valuable source of qualified employees for the future. Nearly half of the interns who have successfully completed the College Intern Program since its inception have found their way back to DADCO, usually after experience elsewhere in the business world.

At about the same time the intern program was launched, DADCO also instituted its Student Investment Program. This program is unique

A Student Investment Class at Washington State University taught by Merilee Frets, a D.A. Davidson & Co. Financial Consultant.

with DAD. It was a brain child of Ian Davidson who conceived it when he was teaching at the University of Montana. It came from his conviction that most college students would be well served in later life by becoming investors in the securities markets. It is based on a premise that an educated buying public will make D.A. Davidson, and all other dealers, more successful than a public which knows little about markets and how they work except what it learns from commercials or the six o'clock news. Ian was convinced that the more investors know about how and why it is important to save, the more they will value and respect the guidance of a skilled and educated counselor. It is the premise which underlies the investment which D.A. Davidson & Co. has committed to the Student Investment Program (SIP) which was, and still remains, one of the more unique partnerships between private industry and public education in the Pacific Northwest, if not the nation.

The first SIP was launched in 1985 at Montana State University at Bozeman. D.A. Davidson & Co. presented the MSU School of Business with $50,000 to be invested in common stocks by upper class students in finance or business. Students are required to do their own research, using such sources of information as are available to any other personal investor—including the research resources at DAD, or other firms. The class decides by consensus what securities are to be bought or sold. An instructor chosen by the school moderates the class. A DAD Financial Consultant acts as an advisor and, if requested, will also serve as an instructor. All transactions are executed through a regular customer account with D.A. Davidson & Co.

Each year, the new class selects its own securities for its portfolio. The results from the year just ended are totalled up, and any profits resulting from the management of the portfolio are shared with the School of Business of each participating institution. If the students have lost money, the loss is absorbed by DAD. Since its inception, participating schools have received in excess of a quarter of a million dollars from their share of the profits generated by DAD's Student Investment Program—and pupils and teachers alike have been exposed to a real-life investing experience, using real money and making decisions which produce real profits—or real losses. It has interjected a hearty dose of reality into what is, too often, academia's theoretical approach to the problems its students will face in the real world.

Currently there are 14 schools in the program— Montana State University–Bozeman, University of Montana, University of Idaho, Washington State University, Carroll College, Montana State University–Billings, Boise State University, Gonzaga University, Brigham Young University, University of Utah, University of Oregon, University

Making an investment in Boise State.

of Washington, Westminster College, and the University of Great Falls who participate in the Student Investment Program. As each joined, it too received $50,000 to invest. To date, the company has $700,000 invested in the Student Investment Program. As DADCO moves aggressively into other population centers in Washington, Oregon and Utah, the program will likely be expanded. It has already yielded tangible positive results for the firm. In mid-1997, a former SIP student from the University of Idaho joined the DAD Research Department as a Research Assistant. The news media is universally enthusiastic about the Student Investment Program in every place where a participating school is located. The favorable recognition the program has engendered has played a major role in establishing D.A. Davidson & Co. as a business that really cares—about the communities in which it does business, about the people with whom it does business, and about its sincere desire to be a good citizen and friend of both. It identifies DADCO as a "different kind of company"—a niche it is eager to occupy.

Technology has vastly increased the amount of knowledge available to consumers, and the speed by which it is transmitted. That fact not only makes it necessary to have a well-educated work force, but also to keep it continually retrained to meet constantly changing conditions. Continuing education is one of the most important elements in the success of any modern business.

DADCO management understands this. Each of its offices is equipped with the latest in technological equipment; and all are linked together with national markets, with corporate headquarters, and with other offices, to supply everyone with timely and complete information to meet the needs of their customers. It maintains a staff of specialists headed by a major corporate officer to train employees in the proper use of the equipment and to provide assistance when problems arise—as they frequently do. Much of the training and trouble-shooting is done at the local level. It requires almost constant travel on their part, but often such "hands-on" service is the only way to assure that the customer will always have the information when he or she needs it.

It is a part of DADCO's effort to merit the distinction as the premier company in its niche.

Modern tools in the hands of people skilled in their use are, however, only the means to an end in any investment program. The end result of any successful financial plan is to create wealth for its owner. The fundamental weakness in the emerging concept of discount brokering is that it tends to minimize or eliminate the expertise of a well-trained financial consultant from the process. It seems to assume, as a basic premise, that all who have money to put away for their future are somehow equipped by nature or instinct with an innate knowledge of how to choose and maintain the investment vehicles which will best meet their needs. They predicate their approach on the assumption that the only service the broker renders is to execute trades; and that the whole area of investment selection is one which should be reserved to the investor alone.

It is a concept that plays to the ego of the investor, but the sorry record of the average American when it comes to handling his or her money belies its validity. The rate at which Americans save for their future is among the lowest of all industrialized peoples. They make more money and save less of it than almost anyone else.

D.A. Davidson & Co. is a company that is dedicated to serving the financial needs of the individual customer. Reasonable charges for executing trades is a part of the service it offers—but only a very minor part. Its major mission is to help the money of its customers grow in value so that they will have the security they need when they need it. Its major job is to help the customer select the best products of the right kind to produce that security. That is where its research services come into play.

DAD has long been a leader in research. It hired its first in-house Chartered Financial Analyst (CFA) in 1975, and research has been one of its major departments ever since. In addition to maintaining an in-house regional research department, it has maintained for many years strong national research relationships with such noted firms as First Boston, Donaldson, Lufkin & Jenrette, and Pershing & Co. They have given the DAD brokers access to research information on hundreds of companies whose shares are traded on national markets. In early 1996, the in-house research activities were consolidated and coordinated with those of Financial Aims Corporation and Davidson Trust Company under the direction of Randall Yoakum, who became DADCO's first Chief Investment Officer. He came to the firm from a St. Louis bank where he supervised the activities of more than 120 analysts managing more than $20 billion of customer assets. It was a tribute to the stature of DADCO in the Pacific Northwest investment community that it was able to attract a professional with the credentials of a Randy Yoakum.

In early 1998, D.A. Davidson & Co. completed the acquisition of

Portland-based Jensen group.

Jensen Securities of Portland, Oregon. Jensen is the acknowledged leader in research covering firms in the Pacific Northwest region and brings a staff of institutional research professionals to the ranks of DAD. When added to its present in-house staff, it puts DAD at the forefront of all firms in the area in its research capability.

A part of the mission of DADCO is to "be *the* premier investment firm in the region." With a work force carefully selected and thoroughly trained, reinforced by a strong program of continuing education, backed by the latest in technology supported in its use by a professional staff of technical experts, and undergirded by a research capability second to none in its region, it is well on its way toward realizing its goal. When coupled with its mission to grow value for its customers, provide a secure and profitable environment for its employees, and be a good neighbor to the communities it serves, it is not hard to understand the reason for its solid and steady growth. It is already the largest regional securities firm headquartered in the Pacific Northwest, and, in the eyes of many knowledgeable observers, already the best.

By following a policy of conservative investing based on the needs and goals of the customer, DADCO has found a niche worthy of its vision.

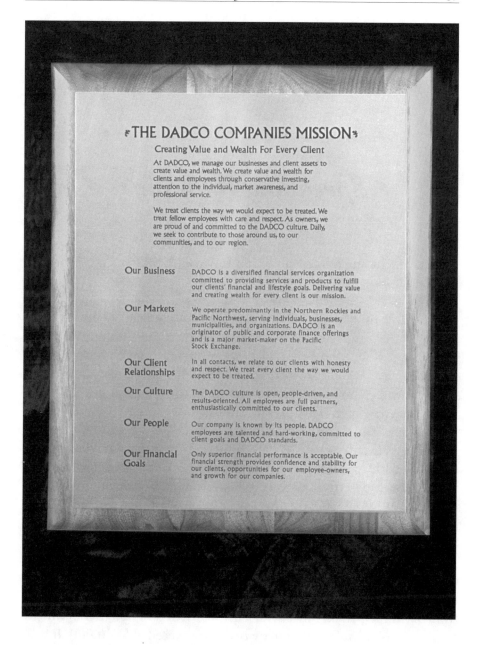

❧THE DADCO COMPANIES MISSION❧

Creating Value and Wealth For Every Client

At DADCO, we manage our businesses and client assets to create value and wealth. We create value and wealth for clients and employees through conservative investing, attention to the individual, market awareness, and professional service.

We treat clients the way we would expect to be treated. We treat fellow employees with care and respect. As owners, we are proud of and committed to the DADCO culture. Daily, we seek to contribute to those around us, to our communities, and to our region.

Our Business

DADCO is a diversified financial services organization committed to providing services and products to fulfill our clients' financial and lifestyle goals. Delivering value and creating wealth for every client is our mission.

Our Markets

We operate predominantly in the Northern Rockies and Pacific Northwest, serving individuals, businesses, municipalities, and organizations. DADCO is an originator of public and corporate finance offerings and is a major market-maker on the Pacific Stock Exchange.

Our Client Relationships

In all contacts, we relate to our clients with honesty and respect. We treat every client the way we would expect to be treated.

Our Culture

The DADCO culture is open, people-driven, and results-oriented. All employees are full partners, enthusiastically committed to our clients.

Our People

Our company is known by its people. DADCO employees are talented and hard-working, committed to client goals and DADCO standards.

Our Financial Goals

Only superior financial performance is acceptable. Our financial strength provides confidence and stability for our clients, opportunities for our employee-owners, and growth for our companies.

DADCO's Mission Statement is prominently displayed throughout the workplace.

Spreading Its Wings

The concluding paragraph in Ian Davidson's master's thesis of July 1956 read:

> "Gibson Associates has potential that is not being realized. If the firm were to increase its present staff, adopt an aggressive sales policy, place more emphasis on non-listed securities and take advantage of regional stock exchange membership opportunities, it would show a great deal of improvement in its present status."

It is a succinctly-stated recipe for success for any regional securities firm—or, with appropriate adaptation, most other types of business for that matter. It describes, with bare-bones simplicity, much of what has happened at DADCO in the years since he wrote it. But with advancing technology and explosive growth, it has, of course, become far more complex than his simple summary would imply.

We have already described how some of Ian's recommendations in his thesis were implemented early after his arrival with the firm. By the time David A. Davidson died in 1970, the firm he founded had grown from one three-person office with a net worth of $33,000 to four offices employing 67 people with a net worth that exceeded $850,000. It was firmly established in its own home in Great Falls; was a member of the two largest regional stock exchanges; had a corps of top-notch field managers; a superb back-office operation; and had already established itself as one of the preeminent retail firms in its field in Montana. It had also taken a first major step toward expanding the scope of its services which would transform it from just a good retail broker/dealer to a recognized full-service financial services firm.

In the mid-1960s, Eugene S. Hufford, a Denver municipal bond underwriter, started to call with some regularity on D.A. Davidson & Co. Prior to that time, the municipal bond business in Montana had been dominated by three Minneapolis firms, led by Stanley Abby of Kalman & Co. In Ian's words, "they were taking a ton of money" out of the state each year. Two of the firms, Piper Jaffray & Hopwood and J.M. Dain & Co. (now Dain Rauscher), also maintained retail brokerage

Gene Hufford

offices in the state. Yet needs for sewer and water mains and treatment plants, streets and bridges, sidewalks and street lighting, and a host of other municipal improvements were as great in Montana as in Colorado or Minnesota. To finance them, municipalities, or subdivisions thereof, frequently borrow money by issuing bonds. A securities dealer buys the bonds from the issuer and resells them to its customers. The price the dealer pays includes the amount required to pay off the bonds as they come due, and a mark-up to cover selling expenses and a profit to the dealer. The bonds are redeemed from the tax revenue of the municipality or subdivision, the revenue from usage fees for service rendered by the improvement, or both.

As an incentive to an individual investor to buy municipal bonds at a price that will keep the cost to the taxpayer as low as possible, the buyer customarily receives special tax treatment. Interest on Montana bonds are exempt from both Montana and Federal income tax. For a state like Montana, with one of the nation's highest state income tax rates, this feature offers an especially attractive investment opportunity.

Municipal bonds fit the needs of many of D.A. Davidson's conservative investors. They also offer local communities with a source of local financing to enable them to upgrade the quality of life for their people. If they can be acquired from a local firm with representatives who live in their midst and know both the community that issued the bonds and the people who bought them, it often make them doubly attractive. To Ian Davidson, this combination made a municipal bond department a natural fit with a firm which had already established a solid reputation as a dealer in quality stocks and mutual funds.

As Ian became better and better acquainted with Gene Hufford, he became increasingly impressed with his competence and professionalism. Discussions between them about a DAD municipal bond department heated up; and in January 1968, Gene Hufford joined DAD to open Montana's first full-service Municipal Bond Department and head its operation. It was an historic first step that would move D.A. Davidson & Co. from a local broker/dealer in securities to a diversified regional conglomerate offering a wide range of financial services throughout a multi-state area in the Intermountain West.

It also presented a new challenge to DAD Registered Representatives (as they were known at the time) who were expected to play a major role in marketing the issues which Gene developed. While stocks and bonds are often regarded as synonymous in the lexicon of the uninitiated, they are far different animals in the way they are structured, the way they are brought to market, and the way they are sold. "My first job when I came to D.A. Davidson was to educate the troops about bonds," Gene recalled. "None of them knew diddly-doo about municipal bonds—including Ian. Sometimes it got pretty frustrating. But Montana did offer some advantages that many of my old colleagues in Denver thought were disadvantages. The Denver market had about two million people and 19 bond dealers. Montana had about 600,000 people at the time with two dealers—including me. It didn't take a rocket scientist to figure out that Montana had about three times more potential customers per dealer than did Denver."

There's that "measuring the market potential" again that Ian had emphasized in his thesis!

"Montana also had another advantage," Gene continued. "It required that municipal bond issues be sold at public auction as opposed to Colorado which allowed such bonds to be sold by negotiation between dealer and the municipality. This assured that in Montana the municipality—and ultimately, the buyer—would receive the best prevailing price. Under a negotiated sale, there was sometimes under-the-table payments or other questionable inducements made, usually to the detriment of the taxpayer."

"What we tried to do," he chuckled, "was to try to build a nine-foot fence around Montana to keep other dealers out."

It was quite successful. At a dinner commemorating his retirement in 1993, it was noted that during his 25 years of service, Gene Hufford had underwritten nearly 80% of all the Montana municipal bond offerings brought to market during his tenure. When asked how he did it, he laughed,

"It was pretty simple. All I did was to drive a hundred miles or so after work to attend some small town school board meeting which usually lasted 'til close to midnight. I then drove home and hit the sack sometime after 2 A.M. so I could get up and be ready for a 6:30 A.M. sales meeting at the office before the market opened—and kept doing it for 25 years."

The formula may be simple, but such performance is pretty rare. Gene Hufford deserves a special place of honor in the annals of DADCO. He not only pioneered the way to its present-day position of preeminence in the financial services field, but he set the standard for excellence enjoyed by DAD's Capital Markets Division today.

In 1975, D.A. Davidson & Co. took a second major step toward its financial services transformation. It is also where my connection with the firm began. We already had a close personal relationship with Ian Davidson. He married our daughter, Nancy, in 1961. But in 1975 we established our first business association with the firm which Ian Davidson now headed.

Five years earlier, I had left the life insurance company with which I had spent more than 40 years to embark on a new venture. Financial planning was a hot new concept in financial services. It was based on the idea that, while there are many ways to *sell* a financial product, the most effective way to *buy* one is to first identify and prioritize the particular personal, family or business need that a particular product must satisfy. Only then is the individual able to select, often with the aid of a knowledgeable counselor, financial products which are specifically designed to satisfy each particular need.

Today, financial planning is widely accepted as a good starting place for long-term financial success. In 1970 it was a radical new idea when, with three associates, I left the life insurance business to start a company we called Financial Aims Corporation, then based in Minneapolis. Our targeted niche was a service offered to major corporations as an employee benefit for top executives. One of our early clients was a major regional securities firm in Minneapolis. It hired us to do financial studies for some of its top people. It also bought an option to purchase a majority interest in our business as an adjunct to its brokerage services. A short time later, however, the CEO retired to pursue new interests, and the firm changed the direction of its priorities. It allowed its option to purchase Financial Aims stock to expire.

This opened the door for Ian Davidson. Because of our personal relationship, he was aware of what was going on in Minneapolis. He

Financial Aims Corporation.

knew that, while our firm was successful enough to convince him that the financial planning concept was sound, it was also new enough that it had not gained broad public acceptance. It was becoming more and more apparent that it would take much longer to develop Financial Aims into a profitable venture than we had first visualized. Like many new businesses, we were under-financed. An association with a growing firm like D.A. Davidson & Co. could be a happy marriage for both firms.

On January 2, 1975, Financial Aims Corporation became the first wholly-owned subsidiary of D.A. Davidson & Co. I returned to Great Falls to head it. For us, it was homecoming. Almost 16 years earlier we had left Great Falls to take a new job with the insurance company in Minneapolis. Now we were returning home to run our own business as a part of a larger family organization.

An unanticipated development which came out of our early studies was a keen interest in financial products which would allow the buyer to minimize or defer taxes. Many of our clients were people with relatively large incomes taxed at very high rates. Any plan that offered those folks some current tax relief gained a ready audience. The problem was that many of the plans which proposed such relief were either based on statutes or regulations which had been untested in court, or were promoted by questionable characters posing as avant-garde pioneers in financial concepts. They were often very convincing, but sometimes not too conscientious.

Many of the popular tax shelters of the early 1970s had backfired by the end of the decade. The courts decided in some cases that the promised tax relief was based on a flawed understanding of tax laws or IRS regulations. The experience did have one positive side effect, however. It forcefully demonstrated the value of knowledgeable management of sizable pools of assets by professionals dedicated to helping their owners achieve pre-determined financial objectives. The niche market for financial planning we had tried to develop in Minnesota proved impractical in a state like Montana where large business organizations with a corps of highly-paid executives were few and far between. As a result, investment portfolio management became a larger and larger part of the Financial Aims business. By the time Bill Macfadden took over in 1981, the subsidiary had become almost exclusively an asset management firm. The financial planning function became largely dormant until later revived under the guidance of the trust company, and more recently, the Professional Development Department under Jim Searles.

By the end of 1998, Financial Aims Corporation was managing well over three-quarters of a billion dollars of client assets and furnished management expertise to another three-quarters of a billion of assets administered by Davidson Trust Co. Jack Davant, a 21-year DADCO veteran, heads both the money management company and the trust company as Chief Executive Officer of both organizations.

Jack Davant

The purchase, almost a quarter of a century ago, of a struggling Minneapolis financial planning pioneer has proven to be a highly profitable addition to the DADCO stable of diversified financial services for many of its 100,000 clients in the Pacific Northwest.

With a municipal bond department and a money management firm well established as profitable adjuncts to its growing retail brokerage network, it became obvious by 1982 that it was necessary to pause to establish a more formal plan for digesting the steps already taken and identifying the ones which would be required in the future if it was to become a complete financial services organization.

The Strategic Planning Conference was born.

The company's first such conference set forth DAD's objectives for the ensuing three years, and outlined the actions necessary to achieve them. A plan was prepared under the guidance of a professional planning firm and involved most of the firm's key people in its development. The strengths of the company were identified, and consensus adopted on the actions which would build on those strengths. Responsibilities were assigned, and timetables set for their completion. The company's weaknesses and shortcomings were analyzed in like manner. As a direct result of its first planning conference, Bruce Madsen, then the Missoula Branch Manager, became Vice

Strategic planning session.

President and Director of Retail Branches. He continued to be headquartered in Missoula. Dick Hughes succeeded him as the manager of the Missoula Branch.

The 1982 Strategic Planning Conference pinpointed the concentration of micro-management duties in top executive officers as a potential barrier to its regional growth. These duties, it advised, should be dispersed among managers at the branch office and department

Bruce Madsen

level. By doing so, top management would be better able to concentrate on initiating steps which would allow it to successfully compete for a share of the financial services market in Spokane, Boise, Salt Lake City, Portland, Seattle, and other urban centers in the Pacific Northwest.

In August 1982, Bruce Madsen became President of D.A. Davidson & Co. and was relocated to the corporate headquarters in Great Falls. Ian Davidson retained his position as Chairman and Chief Executive Officer. Responsibility for the development and supervision of the firm's retail branch office network continued to be the responsibility of Bruce, leaving Ian free to explore and pursue other expansion possibilities.

The second Strategic Planning Conference in 1985 was more extensive than the first and explored in greater detail the strengths and weaknesses which had been identified in the 1982 study. It also confirmed the value of periodic updates on an ongoing basis. These conferences are now an integral part of the DADCO agenda. The revision in 1997 was the sixth since 1982, and plans are already on the drawing board for the next one.

The 1985 Conference coincided with DAD's fiftieth anniversary year and pinpointed several significant milestones to be targeted in the years which followed. It determined that, to be able to deliver the services required from a diversified financial services firm, it must first strengthen its existing capability and shore up those areas which were weak or non-existent. It must also gain industry recognition as a "different" kind of securities firm, capable of delivering a complete line of financial services while still retaining its distinctive personal touch. Establishing specialist posts on the Pacific Stock Exchange seemed to be one way to satisfy both objectives. Such a move would put D.A. Davidson & Co. into the wholesale side of the business, yet would not compete with the retail side where DAD had already established itself as a regional leader. If successfully managed, a specialist operation could provide a source of

Davidson Trust Co.

added revenue which would enable it to expand into mortgage banking, syndicate underwriting, trust services, and other areas.

It was just one week after the 50th anniversary party that the Board of Governors of the Pacific Stock Exchange chose D.A. Davidson & Co. to operate a new Specialist Post on its San Francisco trading floor. The company was awarded the Post in competition with several much larger and better known national firms on the basis of its financial strength and local reputation. DAD had been a member of the Pacific Exchange for 27 years, but it was the first time it had gone head-to-head competitively with some of the industry giants. The David-Goliath aspect of the award caused some in the industry to take a new look at the growing Montana firm

Paul Sweeney was selected to head the new Post #81. Within a year, he had moved it into the top spot among all West Coast Specialist Posts in customer satisfaction, as determined by a quarterly rating system employed by the Exchange. To prove it was no flash in the pan, the Post retained its top rating in each of the succeeding quarters during its first five years. This achievement called further industry attention to DAD.

Since the first specialist post was established in San Francisco in 1985, the Pacific Exchange has awarded D.A. Davidson & Co. fourteen additional posts—nine in San Francisco and five in Los Angeles. It is now the largest specialist operator on the Pacific Exchange. In 1998, its posts handled a trading volume well in excess of 750 million shares and will exceed 1.2 billion shares in 1999. More importantly, every post continues to be highly rated in every customer service evaluation. No longer do firms with whom DAD competes in this segment of the business look upon its record as some sort of an aberration. DAD is accepted as a model when it comes to providing superior service to its customers, and is so recognized among its peers.

The ability to offer trust services was also considered essential for it to be considered a fully-integrated diversified financial services organization. However, the purchase of a trust company presented a whole new set of problems. The purchaser had to comply with a complicated set of state laws governing trust company registration. It also had to provide an orderly way to satisfy the legal requirements of ownership presented by a group of diverse financial services under a single entity. To meet these requirements, the company established DADCO in May 1986 as an independent holding company. The stock of D.A. Davidson & Co. and Financial Aims Corporation was acquired

Ian B. Davidson
Chairman and Chief Executive Officer
DADCO Companies

by DADCO in exchange for stock in the new holding company. Ian Davidson became Chairman and CEO of DADCO as well as D.A. Davidson & Co., with a separate Board of Directors elected to manage the new corporation. D.A. Davidson & Co. and Financial Aims Corporation retained their separate identities as wholly-owned subsidiaries of DADCO, each with its own officers and directors.

With the structure in place which would comply with the law and yet retain the autonomy desired for each component, DADCO acquired Trust Company of Montana in June 1986. Its old friend, Bob Bragg, was chosen its head, and the new acquisition is operated independent of the other DADCO companies.

While it was moving into the specialist post area on the Pacific Exchange, and expanding the scope of its services to include money management and trust services, the company also strengthened its capability in investment banking and in research. We have already noted that DAD had been a leader in the municipal bond business since 1968. Its efforts, however, had been aimed almost exclusively to the Montana municipal market. If it was to compete in a regional arena, it would have to raise its

Mark Semmens

sights and bring on board specialists who were knowledgeable in other investment banking areas. In March 1987, a Corporate Finance Department was established under the direction of Mark Semmens, the former Bond Program Manager for the Montana Economic Development Board. The Municipal Bond Department under Gene Hufford concentrated primarily on Montana municipal issues, while Mark's department was mainly concerned with structuring corporate and other bond issues to meet the capital needs of business and other organizations in the Pacific Northwest.

Gene Hufford retired in 1993. At that time, the Municipal Bond Department was re-organized as Public Finance Capital Markets under the leadership of Kreg Jones, another School of Business graduate of the University Montana. It now has municipal bond underwriters headquartered in Washington and

Kreg Jones

Idaho, as well as Montana.

Mark Semmens continued to head the Corporate Finance Department which has enjoyed a steady growth. It now has investment banking specialists in Spokane, Salt Lake City, Seattle, and Portland in addition to Great Falls. In February, 2000, Mark announced his intention to step down as head of Corporate Finance, to devote more time to the needs of his growing family. He will continue to serve DAD as a Senior Investment Banker. Doug Woodcock, who heads the Institutional Equity operation in Portland, Oregon, will assume the retitled position of Director of Equity Capital Markets. The new alignment will encompass all equity capital market activities, which includes Corporate Finance, Institutional Sales, Equity Trading, and Institutional Research. Because of his close association with DAD's major research center on the Pacific Coast, Doug will maintain his headquarters in Portland. He will continue to serve on the DADCO Board of Directors and on its Management Committee.

To further enhance its image as a financial services firm, and to provide it exposure at the national level, a reorganized Syndicate Department increased its participation in the marketing of new security issues. When a corporation wishes to raise money to start or expand a business, it usually contracts with an investment banking firm to structure a new stock or bond offering and sell it to the public. The principal firm forms a selling group composed of other brokerage firms who agree to buy a part of the new issue and, in turn, sell it to their customers. The role of the Syndicate Department is to develop a relationship with leading investment bankers who are active in the type of offerings appropriate for the kind of customer served by DAD brokers. It also screens the details of the new issues to determine if they are well structured and fairly priced.

DAD had a Syndicate Department since July 1981 when Jerry Milkowski became the first head. When Jerry left in January 1987 to join an East Coast firm, Charles Abernathy was asked to head the reorganized department. Charlie first joined DAD in April 1968 and is the firm's fifth oldest employee in terms of service. A North Carolina native and a graduate of Duke University, he had been stationed at Malmstrom Air Force Base in Great Falls while in military service. There he met and married his wife, Sydne, a childhood friend of Nancy Davidson. After his discharge in 1959, Charlie entered the securities business with Merrill Lynch, Pierce, Fenner & Smith, first in New York City and then in California. When DAD expanded its Great Falls Branch

Office upon its move back to the then-Steele Building, Ian asked Charlie to become its manager. It was the culmination of a long "courtship." After Charlie's discharge from service, the Davidsons and the Abernathys maintained the friendship which started when Charlie and Sydne were married. Charlie had been very successful at Merrill Lynch, and both were quite satisfied with their California lifestyle. However, Ian felt that if the right opening should develop, Charlie could be enticed to return to Sydne's home town, despite the fact that she had let Charlie know—only partly in jest—that she had married him only so she could "get away from Montana and live in New York."

The Great Falls job proved to be a great fit. Charlie built the Great Falls office to a top position in the company and attracted some outstanding associates, many of whom have gone on to occupy other leadership posts in the firm. He and Sydne have also become among the most active community leaders in Great Falls. When Ian needed a top-notch person to head the Syndicate Department, Charlie moved upstairs to the corporate headquarters. He had built well. One of his most able recruits, Bert

Charlie Abernathy

Thurber, stepped in as his replacement in Great Falls without missing a beat. Charlie's previous New York contacts have proven invaluable in his new role, and he has built a profitable unit which is well known in the industry. As the new millennium dawned, Charlie Abernathy elected to wind down toward retirement by relinquishing his duties as head of the Syndicate Department. In March, Marge Sitzmann, a 19 year veteran in Syndicate management, joined DAD as Vice President. She brought with her an impressive record of accomplishments with several major firms, the latest of which is Kirkpatrick Pettis in Omaha.

From its very beginning, D.A. Davidson & Co. has considered both intensive and extensive research to be essential to its long-term success. Because of the inherent Davidson conservatism, it has always leaned more heavily toward fundamental than technical research. For the uninitiated, fundamental research primarily

Marge Sitzmann

Portland Research principals with Bruce Madsen, center, (left to right) Doug Woodcock, Tom Carley, Bob Mitchell, and John Rogers.

Reprint of announcement of Jensen purchase from the Oregonian in Portland.

considers the underlying values of the company issuing the stock or bond in predicting future performance. Technical research relies more heavily on trends in the overall market: which segment of the economy is currently strong and which is weak, political and social trends which may affect future values, and the like. For traders who hope to profit from quick swings in the market, technical factors usually take precedence over fundamentals in predicting whether the price of a stock will go up or down. For the investor wishing to build a solid financial base to meet specific long-term needs, the fundamental approach is likely to better reflect the future performance of a stock or bond over a long period of time—though, technical factors may alter the basic underlying values, and cannot be ignored. Since DAD has, from its very beginning, been more committed to serving the long-term investor than the short-term trader, its research has tended to lean more to the fundamental than the technical in its emphasis.

In the beginning, the company relied on its representatives to do their own individual research, augmented by reports from analysts with outside research firms. However, in 1975, it took its first serious step into in-house research when it hired Bill Thompson, a west coast Chartered Financial Analyst. Bill retired in 1982 and was succeeded by Jim Bellessa, a graduate of Brigham Young University with an MBA and a Chartered Financial Analyst (CFA) designation. Jim brought with him extensive experience as a trust officer and a securities portfolio manager. Under Jim, the department was expanded. Lloyd Rixe, PhD, was added to the staff, and relationships established with some of the most prestigious East Coast research firms in the industry. Bellessa specialized in research on issues of smaller Pacific Northwest firms with good investment potential. He still fills that role, augmented by the Jensen organization which DAD acquired in early 1998.

Jensen Securities is a group of 20 investment analysts, institutional sales representatives, and support group in Portland, Oregon which specializes in research of firms headquartered in the Pacific Northwest. It follows, on a continuing basis, the financial and business ups and downs in more than 85 such firms and provides access to this information, not only to interested DAD customers, but to some of America's largest mutual fund and institutional banking institutions. "When Fidelity (the largest mutual fund company in the industry) wants to know everything about Microsoft or Boeing or Micron, they contact Jensen," explained Vice President Doug Woodcock when queried about Jensen's business.

By the early '90s, the Research Department of D.A. Davidson & Co. had become well-recognized in the local area. Its reports were cited frequently in the state and regional business press. Ian Davidson, together with Jim Bellessa, Lloyd Rixe, and others actively continued the investment seminar program which had been

Jim Bellesa

started in 1964 by Stanley Nabi, and sponsored by local Financial Consultants in each community in which DAD maintains a branch office. These seminars proved to be extremely popular, attracting as many as 250 DAD clients and potential customers to a single session. Many were followed by smaller and more individualized meetings with individual DAD brokers, sometimes consisting of several sessions, and often assisted by representatives from allied fields—insurance, accounting, legal, etc. When Fred Dickson joined DAD in 1993 as Director of Research, he expanded this effort. He also added two highly qualified analysts to his staff and instituted an intern program which has already produced two fully qualified research assistants.

Over the years, as DAD's list of customers has grown, research has become increasingly productive. No longer do its analysts simply read financial reports, or chat with the financial officers of those companies in which DAD's customers own shares of stock to see how a company *has* done. Now, a major part of their time is spent in seeking out and investigating wealth-growing opportunities which may lie in lesser-scrutinized firms with outstanding management and a record of long-term financial success. It then brings these opportunities to the attention of DADCO asset managers who can often fit them to a particular situation for an individual customer or account. As the stock value is discovered by the market and its price increases, so does the client's wealth. It is a formula that has served noted investors like Warren Buffet very well. It hasn't been bad for DAD customers either.

Many of these situations are often ignored by the money managers of the Wall Street giants because they are too small to be attractive or too remote from their seat of power to be conveniently accessible to their analysts. But to a firm like DAD and its customers, it can prove to be an invaluable source of untapped wealth.

Proper insurance coverage is also an essential part of a well-designed long-term financial plan. Contrary to the practice of some financial services organizations, DADCO makes no attempt to operate a full-fledged insurance sales and service unit. Instead, it provides an advisory service through which it can help its clients assess and evaluate the financial risks to which they are exposed, and can help them arrange the proper kind and amount of insurance to meet their needs. Every new financial consultant is licensed to give advice on life and health insurance, as well as annuities, at the time he or she is registered by the NASD. D.A. Davidson & Co. maintains brokerage agreements with several leading life and health insurance underwriters. All DAD people who are licensed to supply insurance advice have access to quality insurance and annuity products for those clients who have need for them.

DADCO insurance activities are directed by John Bebee who also serves as a trust officer with Davidson Trust Co., specializing in pension, profit sharing, and 401(k) administration. John has an M.B.A. degree from the University of Montana and was Chief Deputy Insurance Commissioner for the State of Montana before he joined DADCO in 1987. He must approve all insurance sales agreements made with D.A. Davidson & Co. or any of its financial consultants, establishes insurance guidelines appropriate for DAD clients, and monitors the financial condition of the company issuing the insurance.

It is an arrangement that avoids most of the inherent conflicts of interest that arise when the one selling a financial product also has a direct financial interest in its purchase.

DADCO has Financial Aims to furnish management for its larger clients with specialized investment objectives. But with the proliferation of mutual funds—(there are more mutual funds from which investors can choose than there are stocks offered on the New York Stock Exchange)—choosing the right fund for a customer's particular need requires almost as much information as does the selecting of individual stocks or bonds. Oftentimes, a fund will offer a "family" of choices to meet a variety of financial objectives. Some charge for their service at the time the fund is purchased; others make a charge when it is sold; while still others impose a sales charge only if the fund is liquidated before the end of a certain period of time—typically five to seven years. All impose a management fee paid from the earnings of the fund which reduces its net return.

Buying mutual funds is an ideal way for smaller investors to get desirable diversification in their investing. History provides compelling evidence that, over the long haul, common stocks will earn a greater return than any other type of savings or investment plan. While, as most people are well aware, the price of stocks are subject to big periodic swings, up or down, the general trend in the value of common stocks over the past 150 years has been consistently upward as the economy of America has grown and expanded. But within that general trend, to select and manage a portfolio of stocks which will be sufficiently flexible to meet the future money needs of a particular customer for a particular purpose at a particular time, requires skill and knowledge beyond the scope of the average person. That gave rise to the concept of Managed Assets. It tracks the performance of a whole potpourri of mutual funds in meeting the objectives which the fund is organized to meet. It evaluates the quality of its management. It assesses the background—education, experience, investment philosophy, track record—of the manager(s) of each fund. In this way, it can supply a customer with the information which he or she needs to make a fully informed decision.

Today, DAD's Managed Assets Department is one of the fastest growing areas of the firm. Working under the direction of Jack Davant, President of Financial Aims Corporation, it not only provides research data and establishes investment strategy for the money managers at Financial Aims and other selected outside managers, but it provides DAD Financial Consultants with current in-depth information about mutual funds and their investment managers. It also oversees the administration of DADVISOR and other such WRAP accounts which combines all the costs associated with such accounts into a single fee.

By the end of 1995, most of the pieces were in place to transform D.A. Davidson & Co. from a retail brokerage firm to a diversified, financial services organization capable of delivering quality investment advice and service equal any in its region. It had specialists equipped to meet almost any conceivable financial need — from a complex corporate bond issue or the management of a large trust account, to paying bills for beneficiaries unable or unwilling to handle their own financial affairs. It had installed a network of computer and other electronic equipment to provide almost instantaneous communication between every major securities exchange, between DAD branches, and between individuals in them. Every financial consultant can get instant information about a company whose stock a customer might own or is considering. Its people have the same access to the same information as do any broker or analyst in Wall Street or any other financial center.

It has also installed a staff of specialists to train and support them in the use of the electronic equipment. It is a sad, but true, fact of life that modern technology changes so rapidly that it is often almost out of date before it is installed. Millions are spent on computer software ill-suited to the job it was originally bought to do—or under-utilized because those who use it do not know how to get the most out of it. DADCO maintains a professional staff headed by Donn Lassila whose job is to keep abreast of changes in technology applicable to the financial services industry, and to investigate and recommend changes or upgrades that will improve the company's ability to provide up-to-the-minute information to all who may require it. They also train people in its use, and troubleshoot when problems arise. It is one of the company's busiest departments.

The road from the Berkeley campus of the University of California in 1956 to the corner office in the corporate headquarters of DADCO as it approaches a new millennium has been long and sometimes tortuous. But the route outlined in 1956 was clearly marked and faithfully followed. It has brought that early-day vision to a place where DADCO is poised to challenge all comers for a share of the financial services business everywhere in the Northern Rocky Mountain/Pacific Northwest region.

Spreading the Word

There is an old saying that friends should not discuss religion or politics if they want to remain friends. To this we would add personal wealth, for in present-day society, success, fame, honor and influence are largely defined by the wealth a person owns or controls. Occasionally, an exceptional character like a Mother Teresa, a Mohandus Gandhi, or an Abraham Lincoln appears on the scene and to make us pause to assess true personal worth; but for the most part, money, wealth and position defines a person's status in society.

Someone has defined character as what a man is; reputation is what others think he is. They are not always the same—but seldom is a person with a serious character fault able to permanently maintain an unblemished reputation. Sooner or later a person's character and reputation merge into one—for better or for worse.

The same is true for a company. The character of a business is molded by the character of the people who direct its destiny and those who comprise its work force. The reputation it enjoys depends on the faithfulness with which each person performs the task to which he or she is assigned. The sheer number of people involved often makes it more difficult for a business to establish and maintain a reputation for excellence than for an individual. The bigger the business, the harder it is. A perception of shoddy, careless, or unethical behavior, even if only by one in a minor position, is sometimes sufficient to tarnish the reputation of an entire organization—and, if sufficiently grave, the industry of which it is a part. More and more, it seems, a single case of actual or suspected wrongdoing is assumed, by an overly-suspicious public, to be the normal behavior to be expected from all of the same race, the same social strata, or those who are a part of the same business or industry. One greedy stockbroker bends the rules for personal gain, and all stockbrokers become dishonest money-grubbers, unworthy of trust. A few drunken Indians go on a crime spree, and all Native Americans are tagged as criminal drunkards.

The more successful a person or business becomes, the more cautious and circumspect they must be; for greater is the cost should their reputation be tarnished by an act of actual or suspected deviant behavior.

Ian Davidson, from the beginning of his business career, understood the importance of maintaining an impeccable reputation. It was ingrained in him by his heritage. His business is taking care of other people's money and helping it to grow. While most DAD customers do not put the worship of their money ahead of that of their God, in many cases it runs a close second. When more than 100,000 people entrust upwards of $12 billion—and growing—to the care and nurture of a modest-size investment firm headquartered in a modest-size western community, it is a huge act of faith. Only by observing the highest standards of business conduct can DAD justify that faith. It is an awesome responsibility which Ian and each of his team take very seriously. In 1982, the firm formalized its commitment to a set of principles which would guide its future conduct. They have been revisited, refined, and recommitted six times since.

The Davidson team knew that if DADCO was to grow, it must establish itself among its peers as a firm which provides a wide array of services to clients at a competitive rate of growth. Further, it had to provide services that were unique and geared to some identifiable niche of the market which would set it apart from its competitors. It had already put in place the basic infrastructure to serve the investment needs of the small-town investor. It had established a network of local branch offices equipped with the latest technology to supply prompt up-to-the-minute investment information to rural communities in the Pacific Northwest, many of whom had long been overlooked by the giants of the industry. Its popular public seminars gave customers and others access to carefully researched economic analysis and investment data as a guide to help them in their own investment decisions. It had established one of the strongest financial bases in the industry. Investors who entrusted their money to DAD could be confident that their money was safe and managed with the utmost of care.

The concern which D.A. Davidson & Co. displayed for supplying the investment needs of those in the rural areas of its trade area had established it as a firm who cared deeply about the financial future of

individual investors in small-town America. Its success in operating its specialist posts in Los Angeles and San Francisco demonstrated DADCO's ability to compete and prosper in the fast-paced and sophisticated specialist segment of the urban metropolitan market. The firm had also demonstrated that it was capable of successfully crafting some innovative investment approaches to fulfill unusual customer needs. A special customer stock purchase plan developed for Montana Power Company to enable its customers to also become shareowners in the company; the structuring of a limited issue of bronzes by a well-known western sculptor so that the artist, the C.M. Russell Museum of Western Art and the buyer would all benefit economically as well as artistically—these are but two of several that come to mind. All this did not escape the attention of the national business press and other public relations media.

Curiosity about the Montana investment phenomenon first surfaced early in 1980 when a financial reporter from *Forbes* magazine called one day to chat. Ian's response piqued further interest, and in October he paid a two-day personal visit to the firm. The friendliness with which he was received, and the candor displayed by all with whom he visited so impressed the reporter that, in a glowing article in its October issue, he described D.A. Davidson & Co. as "the Merrill Lynch of Montana" and characterized it as the "quintessential regional brokerage firm." *Forbes'* reporters have continued to maintain contact with the firm. In 1988, it carried a major follow-up story which again recognized DAD as "a leading firm serving the individual investor."

In 1985, Ian Davidson was chosen by *Western Business* magazine as its Executive of the Year for his "company and employee leadership and commitment to community, state, and region." In 1986, *Changing Times, the Kiplinger Magazine* designated D.A. Davidson & Co. as one of the seven leading regional investment firms in the United States. Similar laudatory coverage followed in *U.S. Today* in 1992, *Newsweek* in May 1993, and a special issue of *Big Sky Business Review,* a monthly publication of the *Great Falls Tribune.*

Each of these stories, while deeply appreciated, was unsolicited by DAD; as were several other honors and recognition given to DADCO and to Ian Davidson. But he was convinced that, if the firm was to achieve identity as a major regional player in the securities industry in the Pacific Northwest, its people would have to become recognized as leaders in industry affairs on a much broader stage. Otherwise, it would continue to be regarded only as a "good little firm" as one West Coast competitor patronizingly characterized it. So Ian and others increasingly accepted positions of industry leadership, even though it meant delegating many of their usual DAD responsibilities to others. Ian Davidson was elected to the Board of Governors of the Pacific Stock Exchange in September 1987. The following year he was named a director of the Securities Industry Association, representing the Pacific Northwest Region. He served both organizations with distinction; and in 1992 he was chosen as Vice Chairman of the Pacific Exchange, its highest non-administrative position. He was the first Montanan ever to head a major stock exchange.

His performance in these positions marked Ian Davidson as a leader in his industry in the Pacific Northwest. It also attracted the attention of leaders at the national level. The National Association of Securities Dealers (NASD) is the only body of its kind, sanctioned by Congress to self-regulate its own industry. The Securities and Exchange Commission (SEC), which establishes the rules governing the securities industry, requires everyone who gives advice with respect to the purchase or sale of securities to be registered by, and be a member of, the NASD. The NASD administers the examinations required for registration, supervises and regulates the conduct of securities dealers, investigates complaints, and assesses punishment for violations. In this capacity, it literally holds business life-or-death power over virtually every stockbroker and member firm in the United States.

It also owns and operates the world's largest electronic stock exchange, NASDAQ, whose trading volume in recent years has surpassed that of the New York Stock Exchange.

The NASD is the *creme de la creme* of all bodies which regulate and promote the securities industry. In 1993, Ian Davidson was elected to the Board of Governors of the National Association of Securities Dealers, representing the entire Pacific Northwest. That, in itself, was a signal honor. But two years later, when the chief executive officer of the "good little Montana firm" was chosen to chair the NASD Board of Governors, it confirmed DAD's place as a significant player in the entire securities industry.

Ian Davidson and DADCO had arrived on the national scene in a big way. It was an opportunity to highlight the Montana scenery, lifestyle and culture which Ian was determined to spotlight. In July 1995, he hosted a summer meeting of the NASD Board of Governors at Bigfork, Montana. It was the first time its midyear meeting in July had been held

Members of NASD Board of Governors visit DADCO headquarters on their way to the board meeting at Flathead Lake in 1995. Left to right: John Schmidt, San Francisco; Jim Holbrook, Birmingham, Alabama; Joe Hardeman, President and CEO of the NASD, Washington, D.C.; Rick McDermott, New York; and Ian.

outside Washington, D.C. Board members were officially greeted by the Governor and other dignitaries at an informal reception where they were introduced to the laid-back Montana lifestyle. It was an unforgettable experience for many of the visitors who were totally unfamiliar with western hospitality, not to mention the chance to escape from Washington in July!

Two weeks later, Ian Davidson hosted a similar meeting, also at Bigfork, for the Board of Governors of the Pacific Exchange. It marked the second time the PCX Governors had held such a meeting in Montana. Both drew raves from those who attended.

Thus, in a one-month period in 1995, Ian Davidson was able to introduce his firm and his operating style to more than 100 of the most influential executives in the securities industry, their staff people, and family members.

However, entertaining influential industry figures and introducing them to the DADCO style was nothing new to Ian and DADCO. There had been others before. It was all a part of a carefully-planned effort, not only to expose DAD people to the knowledge and experience these experts could bring to the firm and its customers, but also to showcase DAD to the experts. Stanley Nabi, one of Wall Street's most distinguished analysts, appeared on his first DAD program in 1963. He has made a repeat visit to Montana almost every year since and never fails to make one or more appearances on behalf of DAD while in the state. (It was also at his urging that this book was written.) Robert Stovall, Gail Dudack, Bob Goodman, and Jim Stack, each a frequent panelist on Louis Rykeser's popular PBS *Wall Street Week* program, have headlined DADCO annual meeting agendas, as have such respected economics analysts as Robert J. Froehlich, who has served as the chief investment strategist for several of the largest and most successful mutual funds in the industry. Bob Froehlich is also one of the security industry's most prolific spokesmen, appearing on financial programs of *CNBC, CNN, Fox News, Reuters Financial Television* and the *Dow Jones Investor Network*, among others. He is also widely quoted with regular frequency by such publications as the *Wall Street Journal, New York Times, Barrons, Forbes, Fortune, USA Today,* and *Business Week.*

Edward S. Hyman, chosen by his peers as Wall Street's leading economist in every year for almost two decades, and his ISI Mutual Funds partner, Al Medaugh, are regular visitors to DAD and its branches. They are always generous in contributing to the economic education of Montana investors. Each year six of the largest mutual fund organizations in the nation host a mutual fund/insurance conference at a Bigfork resort for DAD financial consultants in recognition of their contribution to the success of the host firms. Besides, they tell us, they love to come to Montana, and are stimulated by their visit with DAD people.

One of the earliest major public relations efforts was DADCO's "Wall Street in the Rockies" television series. Picking up on its slogan, *Where Wall Street Meets the Rockies,* the format was similar to that of the popular PBS "Wall Street Week" series. The half-hour show was produced in conjunction with Montana State University and presented quarterly to a statewide television audience. The panel of experts customarily consisted of a nationally recognized financial figure, a well-known authority from academia, and two from the Montana business community—one of which was frequently from DAD. The Director of Telecommunications at Montana State University moderated each segment which was produced under the direction of the Corporation for Public Broadcasting. The series was well received. It gave DADCO

excellent recognition in its area.

More recently the DADCO sponsorship of "Wall Street Week" and "Nightly Business Report" serve the same purpose, but reaches a much wider audience with better programming. These programs now originate through the PBS affiliate in Spokane to reach a Pacific Northwest audience rather than through Bozeman to reach a somewhat more limited Montana market. It took DADCO out of the television program production business, yet put the Davidson name before thousands of actual and potential customers on a daily and weekly basis in company with some of the most respected and authoritative figures in the nation's financial services industry.

All these: DADCO's unequivocal commitment to the highest ethical standards in its relationship with its customers, its employees, and the communities it serves; its marketing philosophy which directs its focus to what the customer wants and needs rather than on products it wants to sell; and the willingness of Ian Davidson to work with others in the industry to promote these principles as a standard for the entire industry has propelled Ian to a position of national prominence. It has also given DADCO a stature and recognition unique for a firm of its size; located, as it is, far from the centers of financial power where such sophistication is expected.

It has also gained for that "good little Montana firm" further recognition as the premier regional financial services firm in the Pacific Northwest—a goal first publicly announced by Ian Davidson at the firm's

50th anniversary celebration—but his secret dream since he wrote his master's thesis at Berkeley a half century ago.

Public awareness of DADCO was, however, only half the job that needed doing. It also had to keep constantly before each member of its growing workforce an awareness of his or her role in its development; and to keep reminding them of the DADCO culture and the part each plays in maintaining it. One of its earliest efforts to do this was a four-page newsletter which Sheldon McKamey, its first editor, called *The Exchange*. At first, its content was largely limited to reporting personal happenings—marriages, births, weddings, promotions, and the like—in the lives of DAD people, plus a report on company events of general interest. The first issue reported the opening of what was to be the ill-fated Williston, North Dakota branch office; the Montana Power stock offering to its customers (referred to earlier); and the selection of Bill Beaman, then Helena Branch Manager, as an "Outstanding Young Man of America" for his community service work. *The Exchange* has grown to be a 32-page publication, published quarterly, and produced by a staff of four, headed by Darlene Miller, DADCO Director of Communications.

Darlene Miller

The general format has changed very little since its start. About half the content of each issue reports corporate news and news of general interest. The other half is devoted to those items of personal interest which took place in each branch or department since the preceding issue. The latter are reported, and largely written, by someone designated in each unit to do so. In layout and presentation, however, it is worlds ahead of the modest four-page publication which first appeared in 1982. Today, the general stories are selected and written by a professional journalist who serves as the firm's media coordinator and is assembled under the direction of a gifted graphic artist, also with professional newspaper experience.

The Exchange is one of the company's most important ways in which it communicates with employees—and which it shares with selected friends of DADCO, both within and without the industry.

One of the hallmarks of almost all DADCO advertising is to feature the quality of its people. Not only does this recognize the contributions

of each employee to the success of the firm, but it also keeps before the public the quality of the people who make up the DAD workforce. The law requires every publicly-owned business to make an annual report of its financial condition to each of its shareholders. In its very early years, DAD reports consisted largely of distributing copies of the statement prepared by the company's auditors to the handful of shareholders who owned company stock. In 1967, however, D.A. Davidson & Co. included the picture of every one of its employees, with a brief job description of each, in that year's annual report. It attracted a great deal of attention to the value of this growing business to their respective communities.

In 1980, DAD began its practice of publishing both an annual and a mid-year report. The mid-year report still continues the practice started in 1967. It features a picture of each employee by branch or department, along with the report of the company's financial status. The annual report, issued as soon as possible following the close of the company's fiscal year at the end of September, reviews corporate growth and results as well as to recognize outstanding accomplishments by associates either for their work with the firm or industry, or for service to their communities or others. It is professionally prepared and contains pictures, graphs, and illustrations of the highest quality, as well as simple and straightforward financial information. Its quality has been recognized by industry organizations as outstanding among its peers.

A unique feature of DADCO's employee relations program has been its People Book. First published in 1983, at the suggestion of a number of its key people, the People Book is a directory of employees, arranged in alphabetical order, together with a short biographical sketch of each. The sketch contains information concerning the date each joined the firm, their job description, education, prior employment, organizations to which they belong, hobbies of both the employee and their spouse, and other family data.

The employee's picture accompanies the biographical sketch.

The People Book also provides each employee with a short history of the firm, recognizes distinguished retirees, and lists significant milestones in its progress. It is updated periodically to reflect new people coming on and those who have left the firm because of retirement or other reasons. It is a communication tool that has done much to promote an appreciation of the DADCO culture among employees and enhance the stature of DADCO as a quality company composed of quality people.

Another effective public relations feature has been Nancy Davidson's annual Christmas message included with the company's annual report. It came into being almost by accident. One of Nancy's hobbies is calligraphy. In 1980, shortly before the annual report went to press, Ian asked Nancy on the spur of the moment one evening if she could prepare an appropriate holiday greeting to be included in the mailing. She found a short poem which she reproduced in calligraphy. It was an instant hit, and a tradition was born. Since the first one was published in 1980, Nancy has composed an original message which is included, not only with the annual report, but also as the firm's expression of appreciation to thousands of customers, shareholders and friends.

In the years since, both Nancy and DADCO have received many enthusiastic comments about her Christmas messages. She has had repeated requests from others to use them for their own purposes. While none of her original poems are directly related to business, they do reflect the values which undergird its foundation.

Nancy Davidson's Christmas messages have become one of DADCO's most effective public relations instruments.

Of all the ways that DADCO has become well and favorably known, however, the most effective has been the involvement of its people in their respective communities. They run the gamut from high-visibility political posts to serving as scoutmaster for a Boy Scout troop to teaching a Sunday school class in their church. Gary Buchanan, Billings manager, served as Montana's first director of the Department of Commerce; Jeff Nesset as Mayor of Lewiston, Idaho; and Brad Dugdale spearheaded a Chamber of Commerce effort to successfully earn distinction as an All-American City for two different cities—Butte, Montana and Coeur d'Alene, Idaho. Jim Wolfe of the Boise branch officiates Big Sky football games; Bob Blakey, Lewiston, and his wife spend several weeks each year working as volunteers in a charity hospital in Haiti as a part of the program of their church; and Todd Preston, Billings, Bert Thurber, Great Falls, and Scott Wink, Havre, are among many who have served their communities as school board trustees.

Community service has been a part of the DADCO culture since its earliest beginning. In a scrapbook prepared for DAD's 50th anniversary observance, there is a picture of Ian Davidson, as the event's co-chairman, delivering tickets for a concert by the U.S. Navy Band to students of

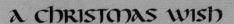

A CHRISTMAS WISH

CHRISTMAS IS the miracle of hope
and understanding• the festival
of friendship• the simple act of sharing.
MAY YOU DISCOVER
the joy in giving• the love in sharing•
the peace in living each day with hope.——
BLESSINGS TO YOU at Christmas
...ways.

Nancy Davidson 1981

A Christmas Prayer

Lord, we see our world
in tension and fear;
give us the courage
and understanding
that we will bring about peace.

Lord, our days are filled
with endless holiday tasks;
help us pause
and listen
to the message of Christmas
that we will use our time
to care for others.

Lord, the burdens of life
cause us hurt and pain;
let the miracle of Christmas
touch us
that we will look forward
to each new day
with joy.

Take care of us
and our fragile world, Lord;
give us the will and compassion

Christmas 1983

Take time
to feel hope at the dawning of day
to find faith through God's gentle way
to give joy to a friend who's alone
to remember, let your heart come home.

Take time
to see wonder in a child's eyes
to seek peace from starlit skies
to be touched by others who care
to love, to laugh, to share.

Take time – for it is Christmas

N. Davidson

D·A·DAVIDSON & CO·

Peace be unto you

In this
blessed season
of love
we wish you
the joy of caring,
the serenity of faith,
courage born of hope,
and peace of a contented heart.

n. davidson

Merry Christmas
1984

D.A. Davidson & Co.

Nancy Davidson

Christmas Prayer

We thank you, Lord, for Christmas, for
understanding the purpose of Christmas
strengthens our faith,
experiencing the miracle of Christmas
gives us hope,
learning the meaning of Christmas
teaches us love,
discovering the essence of Christmas
shows us how to live.

How blessed we are, Lord,
because of Christmas
your gifts of Faith...

May we use these gifts...
in the true spirit of Chr...

N. Dav...

Merry Christm...
DADCO
1991

CHRISTMAS 1998

BELIEVE IN THE MIRACLE OF CHRISTMAS,
For God gives you the Gift of His Son.
BELIEVE IN THE MYSTERY OF CHRISTMAS,
Where God calls you as one of His own.
BELIEVE IN THE MEANING OF CHRISTMAS,
For God loves you and wants you to know
He'll bless you and keep you
Guide you, be with you
This day and all your life long.

christmas prayer

IT'S BEEN 2000 YEARS LORD
SINCE YOU SENT US YOUR SON
HE CAME THAT WE'D KNOW LOVE
AND HOW LIFE SHOULD BE DONE

AFTER 2000 YEARS LORD
WHERE DO WE STAND
HAVE WE CARED FOR EACH OTHER
HAVE WE CARED FOR YOUR LAND?

FOR 2000 YEARS LORD
YOU GUIDED US ON
YOU'VE ALWAYS BEEN WITH US
AS THE YEARS PASSED ALONG

WE'VE HAD 2000 YEARS LORD
TO LEARN LESSONS AND GROW
BE GENTLE AND PATIENT LORD
WE'VE YET A LONG WAY TO GO

THIS CHRISTMAS IS SP...

CAN YOU BELIEVE THE BEAUTY OF WILDFLOWERS
or the vastness of the midnight sky

CAN YOU BELIEVE THE COLORS IN A SUNSET
or the music of a Meadowlark's cry

CAN YOU BELIEVE THE DEVOTION OF FRIENDS
who always beside you stand

OR THE UNEXPECTED ACT OF KINDNESS
that comes from a stranger's hand.

CAN YOU BELIEVE THE TRUST OF A CHILD
as intently he looks into your eyes

OR THE UNFAILING LOVE OF GOD
as we live out His gift of our lives.

GOD'S WORLD AND HIS PEOPLE ARE GOOD
despite hatred and violence and pain

AND THE YEARLY MESSAGE OF CHRISTMAS
is to believe in that goodness again.   n. davidson

Christmas 1996
DADCO

the state school for the deaf and blind. The concert was sponsored by the Junior Chamber of Commerce; the tickets were furnished by Ian's firm; and the picture appeared in the *Great Falls Tribune*. The date was October 5, 1959, and the caption in the scrapbook reads: "Public Service Starts."

Public service at DADCO goes back a long way. Over the years it has manifest itself in many forms: a community theatre renovation in Butte; a statewide high school band festival in Coeur d'Alene; an Honors College home at the University of Montana; an Access to the Arts program sponsored with the Spokane Symphony to provide donated musical instruments to disadvantaged children; and many, many others. The top recognition accorded a DADCO employee each year is the Bragg-Lewis-Knutson Community Service Award. It is given as a memorial to three major DADCO executives who lost their lives in a company plane crash in 1994. It honors their dedication to community service and recognizes the employee each year who best exemplifies their example.

The award is made each year in connection with the DADCO annual meeting.

All this has not gone unnoticed. In 1993, the United Church of Christ honored D.A. Davidson & Co. with its Award for Outstanding Social Responsibility. It was one of eight American corporations so honored for charitable contributions and service to their communities. DAD's nomination was made by the pastor of the local church of which David A. Davidson was a lifetime member.

Again, in 1997, DADCO was the recipient of the Montana Family Business of the Year Award from the School of Business of Montana State University. It was recognized for its growth, its commitment to serving the communities in which it does business, and for creating a corporate culture which "extends your concept of family to include all employees." The award, one of three made each year, was for firms in the Large Employee Category.

As Ian Davidson approaches the start of a new millennium, the reputation of the firm he has guided for forty years is secure among its peers. It has established itself as a good corporate and community citizen. It has had an unbroken record of profitability during the entire period, and its customers and the places where they live have shared handsomely in its success. It is poised for further growth in the region it serves, and anticipates no change in the philosophy of its management which would alter the course of its commitment to excellence which has brought it to its present pinnacle of success.

Investment pays off

Tribune photo by Wayne Arnst

Nancy and Ian Davidson stand at Central Avenue, on the south side of Davidson Court. They will receive the annual Community Livability Award tonight for the court and nearby Circle Plaza.

Davidsons win Livability Award

By JACQUIE BURCHARD
Tribune Staff Writer

The new Davidson Court and Circle Plaza have dramatically changed the look of downtown Great Falls, helping refurbish a key business area and adding the city's first skywalk.

The work hasn't gone unnoticed. Ian and Nancy Davidson will be honored tonight for their investment in downtown.

The city and county commissioners are jointly recognizing the Davidsons as the 1998 recipients of the Community Livability Award.

The award will be presented at the city commission's regular meeting at 7 tonight in the Civic Center.

City officials said the award recognizes the Davidsons for their creativity, vision and dedication.

"Each year, we try to pick someone who has done something to make our city more beautiful and livable, and the Davidsons certainly have," Mayor Joan Bennett said.

Davidson Court and Circle Plaza, dedicated last December, include a landscaped area for community gatherings and off-street parking.

The portion of 3rd Street between Central Avenue and 1st Avenue North has been closed to allow pedestrian traffic only, and a pedestrian walking area and landscaping have been added.

That portion is topped by a glass skywalk and copper-roofed clock tower that stretches between the Davidson Building and Liberty Center.

Beyond the Borders

The distinctive feature that set DAD apart from its peers in its early development was what can best be described as the personal touch. Ian Davidson and his associates regarded each customer as a friend to whom they owe a special obligation. Each became acquainted with the other on a personal as well as a business basis. They were always there to help the customer work through together any problems which might arise before or after any transaction, even some not directly related to business. It was a relaxed relationship, devoid of pressure, and based on mutual trust and respect between broker and client.

It was fairly easy to establish such a relationship in a small community where people know each other, shop at the same stores, or see each other frequently at church, the service club, or at social events. Most of Montana is composed of just such towns. It is a part of the charm of the Big Sky lifestyle.

The personal touch works well in a predominantly rural area which makes up most of Montana, Wyoming, and the Idaho Panhandle. Most of their communities are relatively small. Their inhabitants are not far removed from the pioneer days of the old West when people were forced to rely on one another for their very survival. But transporting such a style to a sophisticated urban center was another matter. Whether a down-home country approach, well received in a Havre, Montana or a Lewiston, Idaho would work in a Salt Lake City or a Seattle was still untried and untested. There were also other differences. Even though the personal touch proved to be universally appealing, the culture of the community, the way people earned their living, and the lifestyle of the area often gave rise to a whole new set of economic and personal needs and desires. Life was less inter-related and therefore, less personal. People could live for years in a big city and never know their next door neighbor. Commuters often knew little about the guy or gal at the next desk or at the next work station. They depended, for their own financial security, on their pension and other benefits from their work, often dictated by employment or labor contracts which they had no personal part in negotiating. To adequately meet the future financial needs of people living in this kind of environment, a financial services firm must be able to offer more solutions than just stocks, bonds, insurance, or other specific products to meet specific needs. It must be able to offer an integrated potpourri of products melded into one cohesive plan specifically tailored to produce the required results at the proper time. By doing so, a company could develop long-term clients rather than spot buyers.

Further, the pensions on which they depended, the businesses for which they worked, and the communities in which they lived needed more and more expert and caring guidance in order to assure that the security on which these people relied would be there when it was needed. All this cried out for the kind of professional financial guidance which a company like DADCO, with it customer-oriented culture, was in business to provide.

However, to actually be able to do so, DADCO had to expand its ability to deliver the guidance promised.

From the time Ian Davidson had joined his father in 1959 and opened the first branch office in Helena, through 1980 when the firm opened its first out-of-state branch in Williston, North Dakota, the expansion effort was largely confined to increasing a retail marketing presence in Montana. During that time, it had established eight branches, put into place a department to structure and sell Montana municipal bonds, acquired a financial planning organization, and increased its net worth from $33,000 to $4.6 million. It had perfected the technique for establishing successful retail stock brokerage offices in a semi-rural area. Even a lackluster Williston experience had provided a valuable learning experience. Had DAD management decided to stop there, as some urged, and be content with what they had successfully built, it would still have been an outstanding success story. However, this undoubtedly would have meant that, at some point in the future, the challenges of new technology and economies of size offered by the diversified, full service concept would have compelled DAD to become a part of such a conglomerate to remain competitive in the marketplace. It is likely that it would have lost its unique culture in the process. This was not a part of the long-range plan of Ian Davidson and the majority of his management team. They decided to press on. The next step, therefore, was to concentrate on expanding the scope of its services before attempting to move into the major urban centers in the region.

Ian was convinced that people the country over would embrace the DADCO style if given the chance. However, his innate Scottish conservatism dictated that he approach the new challenge with extreme caution. The cost in time and facilities to test his conviction required a major commitment of company resources. The Strategic Planning Conference in 1982 was the first step.

As a result of decisions recommended by the 1982 Conference, Bill Macfadden was shifted from Executive Vice President of D.A. Davidson & Co. to President of Financial Aims Corporation to fill a slot created when I retired. It was then that its emphasis shifted from financial planning to money management. At the time Bill took over, Financial Aims managed just over $10 million of customer assets. When he retired in November 1990, assets under its management had grown to more than $130 million and Financial Aims had established itself as a leader in the Pacific Northwest in professional money management.

While the major emphasis during the 1980s had been on the expansion of services, expansion of the retail branch offices system was not neglected. We have already noted the opening of an office in Williston, North Dakota in September 1980—DAD's first branch outside of Montana. At that time, oil drilling activity in the Williston Basin was at its peak and DAD hoped to participate in the resulting economic boom. With the subsequent easing of the Middle East oil embargo, the oil boom

Vinney Purpura   *Bruce Madsen*   *Bob Braig*

in western North Dakota and eastern Montana faded, and the Williston area returned to dependence on its up-and-down agricultural economy for its economic viability. Two years later, in 1984, D.A. Davidson & Co. opened an office in Moscow, Idaho, followed shortly thereafter with the purchase of a Shearson American Express office in Lewiston. When it opened a third office in Coeur d'Alene in early 1986, it irrevocably committed itself to a westward expansion. The Williston office was closed and Jeff Nesset, its manager, transferred to Lewiston to head that office. Jeff has become one of DADCO's shining lights. Not only has he built a successful branch office operation, but he currently serves on the DADCO Board of Directors.

In 1991, D.A. Davidson & Co. also had the opportunity to acquire small offices in Gillette, Cody and Jackson, Wyoming from Dean Witter Reynolds who had decided that offices in small rural areas did not fit with the rest of their business.

This expansion activity was not without its problems and setbacks. None, however, caused more than a momentary pause—and each was a valuable learning experience for future decisions. We have mentioned the Williston failure. It was largely due to an error in evaluating the soundness of the long-range economy of its trade area. To a lesser degree, the same thing happened in the Moscow-Coeur d'Alene area. After a few years of marginal growth, it was apparent that the market would not support three full-service branch offices located within the radius of less than 100 miles of each other—particularly if the major expansion anticipated in the Spokane area became a reality. So the company closed its Moscow branch in 1988, and consolidated its functions with those of the branches in Lewiston and Coeur d'Alene. The move was made with virtually no loss in personnel and proved to be a wise decision in light of the resulting growth in both of the remaining branches. As business expanded and DAD became firmly established as a main player in the securities industry in its niche, the Moscow office was reopened in 1997 as a satellite of the Coeur d'Alene branch to serve the panhandle area of northern Idaho. It suggests that sometimes it is the timing, not the original decision, that is wrong.

Late in 1989 DADCO suffered a minor setback of another nature. It lost two of its long-time stalwarts, one to what proved to be an extended leave of absence, and another to retirement. In October, 1989 Bill Macfadden gave notice of his intention to retire after 30 years of outstanding service. As a prelude, Bill moved up to Chairman of Financial

Aims to make way for Gene Lewis to become its president and chief executive officer. He stayed on to provide support for Gene until November 1990 when his retirement became official. It was typical of the unselfish dedication which Bill Macfadden had given to the firm during 30 years of its existence. When the final chapter of DADCO is written, he will remain as one of the principal architects of its unique culture in the industry.

The second setback was the unexpected resignation of Bruce Madsen as president of D.A. Davidson & Co. Bruce Madsen is another of the team assembled by Ian Davidson who played a major role in transforming DAD from a local, small-town stock brokerage office to the diversified, full-service financial services organization it has become. In this, he joins the likes of Johan Miller, Bill Macfadden, Bob Braig, Gene Hufford, and many, many others—whose willingness to dedicate themselves to a vision and a mission under the inspired leadership of Ian Davidson has made it possible for Dave Davidson's three-person office in Great Falls, Montana to grow into one of the largest, most respected, and most successful businesses of its kind in the region which it serves.

Bruce Madsen first joined DAD in December 1968 as an investment executive in Missoula, his home town, where his family were prominent long-time citizens. He left Missoula to study medicine at the University of Oregon; but, being a "people person," decided his true talents lay in an area which would directly involve more of an interplay with others. He is a master salesman, an excellent athlete who loves to golf and fly fish, and a person who demands perfection from himself and from those with whom he works or plays. A big man, his forceful and charismatic personality tends to dominate any group of which he is a part. With Bruce, you are never in doubt as to where you stand. Yet, around his small son, Owen, he shows a gentleness and tenderness which belies the rough exterior he often tries to project to others. Aside from Ian Davidson, few, if any, have contributed more for more years to the growth of DADCO than has L. Bruce Madsen.

All this seemed to come to a screeching halt, however, when, at the end of November 1989, Bruce Madsen suddenly announced his resignation as the president and chief operating office of DAD. Twenty-one years of relentless drive had taken its toll. He had a severe case of corporate burnout, acerbated by a deteriorating marital relationship. He decided to take a breather from the work force, go to New Zealand for some extended fly fishing with his wife, a passion which they shared, and to reassess his personal goals.

Ian and the Board were understanding and the parting was friendly and cordial. It did, however, necessitate a major realignment of DADCO top management structure. Again, Bob Braig was asked to help fill a breach. He became Director of Retail Branches. The dictionary defines the word "quintessential" as "the most perfect manifestation of a person or thing." In many ways, Robert A. Braig is the quintessential DADCO associate. Born and raised in the Flathead Valley of northwestern Montana, he has never strayed more than 250 miles from his roots. He was educated at the University of Montana with a BA degree in Business. As we reminisced about those early days, he recalled that he "graduated on a Friday in the Spring of 1964. The following Monday I started with D.A. Davidson & Co. in Great Falls as a dividend clerk. I was recommended to Ian Davidson for the job by a Sigma Nu fraternity brother, Warren Drew, who had started working for the firm a short time before. The office was located in the old Great Falls National Bank and I started to study almost immediately for my registration as a broker. In the meantime, I wrote by hand and mailed all the dividend checks to customers."

As we talked, he remembered his first DAD Annual Meeting in 1964. It was held around a table in the coffee shop of the Rainbow Hotel across the street from the office. There were 12 DAD people in attendance—and Bob was able to name them all to me from memory almost 34 years later! Bill Finnerman, an executive from the Pacific Stock Exchange, was the guest speaker, he recalled.

When the Missoula Branch was opened early in 1965, Bob returned to the Garden City with Warren Drew as its initial staff. "We didn't have the fancy fixtures and equipment that Elliott Dybdal and his people provide new offices today," he observed. "We had to fix it up our own. We all pitched in to paint and fix it up so it would project the image of quality we wanted our business to have. But, you know, I think that was probably where the DADCO Culture was born. We felt it was our company. We were proud of it. We wanted our customers to feel a pride in doing business with us."

Later, when DAD bought the Birr Wilson office in Kalispell, Bob Braig returned home to build it into one of the firm's showcase offices in the entire system.

Over the years since, Bob has served as a regional director of branches when D.A. Davidson expanded into the Idaho Panhandle, and as Director of Retail Branches for the period after Bruce Madsen resigned as president in 1989 until Bob Retz was hired in 1991. He has served as a DADCO Director, and was a qualifying member of the Chairman's Council for many years until he started to ease off in his business activity. In recent years, he and his wife, Bev, divide their time between the Flathead and their "fun-in-the-sun" home in Palm Springs. Bob is a master craftsman who has personally built two log homes, and the furniture to go in them, as the time he could spare permitted, first from the demands of a very successful career, and, more recently, from his self-appointed task of monitoring his son, Robbie.

As he summed up our visit, he said, "I guess that if I were to try to describe D.A. Davidson & Co. in one word, it would be 'integrity'—integrity from top to bottom. 'What's best for the customer' has been instilled in every person in the firm—and has been from Day One. It is what has made DAD unique, and no one wants to let it down. We all know that if it isn't good for the customer, it isn't good for us. Everyone accepts it, and tries to live by it."

Greg Barkus, who had been a Conrad, Montana banker before joining DAD in Kalispell, succeeded Braig as Kalispell's Branch Manager.

Finding the right person to fill the job of president of D.A. Davidson & Co. was a bit more difficult. Fueled by an unwise haste to get on with its agenda, the Board turned to a former executive officer of A.G. Edwards and Sons, Guy C. Blackwell. He was elected president in February 1990. Blackwell had been outstandingly successful as a personal investor and came from an organization which shared many of DAD's cultural values. But he had suffered a serious accident which had triggered his resignation at Edwards, and it was soon apparent that his physical problems, coupled with some differences with his colleagues in his investment philosophy, were inconsistent with the DADCO culture. He resigned after only five months on the job and returned to Nevada where he had retained his legal residence. It was a tacit admission that his selection had been a trial run.

Now it was back to square one. This time, the Board looked inward. Vincent M. Purpura had come to D.A. Davidson & Co. in June 1976 as Manager of Operations under Stu Nicholson. A native of Buffalo, New York and educated at New York University—Buffalo, he had held a similar position at Hugh Johnson & Co. in Buffalo. As DAD had grown and Stu became increasingly involved it its overall financial management. Vinney's managerial and organizational skills became more and more evident. He was a superb motivator who commanded the respect of all with whom he worked. He became an ardent champion of the DADCO culture. So, when Vinney Purpura became DAD's fifth president and third chief operations officer, the selection was widely acclaimed throughout the company. His selection has proven to be a stroke of genius. In 1998, Vinney was promoted to Chief Executive Officer as well as President of D.A. Davidson & Co. It was the first time that position had been filled by someone outside the Davidson family.

The story of how Vinney Purpura, a life-long New Yorker who loved the East Coast lifestyle and culture, with a job which was satisfying and secure, wound up in a small western community with a securities firm which, to that time, was virtually unknown in the sophisticated circles of Wall Street, is a story in itself. It is another glimpse into the leadership style of Ian Davidson.

As Vinney tells it, the journey started with a phone call from a gentleman who identified himself as Ian Davidson of D.A. Davidson & Co. (Vinney emphasized the word "gentleman" and used it repeatedly in his further comments.) Ian explained that Vinney had been recommended by several references, whom he was not at liberty to identify, as a person with the qualifications he was looking for as a Manager of Operations in his expanding brokerage firm in Great Falls, Montana. "Neither the name, D.A. Davidson, nor Great Falls, Montana were familiar to me," Vinney said, "and since I had had other such approaches—mostly from one-horse bucket shops selling mostly penny stocks—I was quite cool to the call. However, the voice on the other end was so gracious, so open and candid with its answers to my questions, that I almost felt I owed its owner the courtesy of an interview. I was happy with my present job and was not looking for any change, but when, late on a Saturday night, after the plane, for which the firm had sent me tickets to Great Falls and return, was two hours late arriving, I was met personally by Ian Davidson and spent until 4 A.M. drinking coffee and becoming inundated with his enthusiasm and excitement about the kind of company he was striving to build, I decided I wanted to become a part of it. Here, indeed, was something far different from what I had experienced in the parochial East Coast culture. It was a radical change for me and my family, both in business culture and personal lifestyle. The latter, in particular, took some getting used to, but every day I am thankful to Ian and those references who recommended me. It has been one of the greatest experiences any man could have had."

It is a further testament to the character of Ian Davidson that Vinney's references, given in confidence, have never been revealed.

Vinney Purpura has become the epitome of what DADCO Culture means. He enjoys the trust and respect of customers and employees alike. That 1976 phone call has paid excellent dividends for Vinney and DAD alike.

In 1991 Robert M. Retz, one of Dain Bosworth's outstanding branch managers, came over to DAD to fill the position of Director of Retail Branches, succeeding Bob Braig who had been serving on an interim basis since the resignation of Bruce Madsen. Retz had some long-range retirement plans of his own, but agreed to stay with DAD for at least five years.

As a prelude to an intensified expansion into the urban center of the Pacific Northwest, several changes were made in branch office management. This followed some recommendations first pinpointed in the 1985 Strategic Plan. It is a tribute to the value of the DADCO culture that every managerial change was made with the full cooperation of the existing manager, and every one of the replaced managers is still with DAD and a contributing part of the organization.

The first twenty-five years of life for DAD and its predecessor firm were spent establishing its reputation and defining its character as a respected part of the local Great Falls investment community. It had become known and recognized as a firm with an impeccable reputation in its dealings with its customers and conservative in its investment philosophy. The Davidson family was widely known for their community involvement. Dave Davidson, however, had shown little interest in expanding its influence beyond his local community.

The start of DAD's second twenty-five years, however, coincided with Ian Davidson's arrival on the scene. While there was never any overt clash between Ian and his father, it was clear from the start that Ian did not share his father's comfortable conservative parochialism. His MBA studies convinced him that, in an economic environment about to undergo drastic change, DAD's old ways simply could not be sustained. Substantial capital investments in stock exchange memberships, added clerical staff, and an expanded sales force would have to be made if it were to survive as a viable business in the future. The expenditure involved made this anathema to Dave. But the force of Ian's logic and the soundness of his conclusions prevailed. Ian had done his homework well when he prepared his master's thesis. Time has certainly proved him right.

By the end of its first half century, DAD was prepared to move well beyond its borders as a parochial Montana retail stock brokerage shop. It had done the same kind of in-depth study and planning to shape its plunge into regional diversified financial services that Ian had done to prepare his father's firm for survival and growth within a single community. It had moved beyond its geographical border with its entry into the specialist markets on the Pacific Stock Exchange. It had also built is first blueprint for the integration of the diverse services. It had made the necessary investment in outstanding professional personnel in each of the new areas. It had clearly defined the niche it aspired to occupy in its region; and it had laid the foundation for the culture which would—and does—define the organization.

It was now ready to move out into the larger and more challenging urban arena of the Pacific Northwest and northern Rockies. It was also destined to put the DADCO culture to its acid test.

PART III

A Time of Testing

In 1988, a *Forbes Magazine* editor concluded a follow-up to an earlier story about D.A. Davidson & Co. with this comment: "Davidson is looking for expansion opportunities across the Northwest. After all, if you look at a map, Spokane is just across Idaho from Kalispell." It was an outsider's prescient recognition of a logical expansion which DADCO management had already discussed in its 1985 Strategic Plan. At that time there was a lot of infrastructure to be put in place before it was ready to launch the kind of aggressive effort that such an expansion required.

By the early 1990s, however, DADCO appeared ready. Vinney Purpura was firmly established as President and Chief Operating Officer of D.A. Davidson & Co. and he had his team well in place. Bob Retz had come over from Dain Bosworth as Director of Retail Branch Offices. With Gerry Meyer, a seasoned recruiter and trainer, they made a dynamic trio, well equipped for an aggressive effort to move into new areas. Gene Lewis and Bob Bragg had developed an effective team approach to money management on both an individual and corporate level and had successfully field-tested their techniques.

Strong new branch management was in place in Bozeman, Havre, Billings and Missoula. The firm now operated six specialist posts on the Pacific Stock Exchange, and the trust company had expanded its services into the Kalispell area.

So all systems appeared to be go in June 1992 when DAD announced the opening of its first branch office in the state of Washington. It seemed well poised to start its move into major urban centers.

Spokane was the first location chosen. It was a logical choice. Not only was it the closest urban center to the corporate headquarters in

Spokane's Office.

Great Falls, but it had much in common geographically and economically with those locations in which DAD had already enjoyed great success. While home to some major industrial and manufacturing businesses, Spokane also relied heavily on a strong agricultural economy for its prosperity. It was, in a sense, a big small town, the kind in which DAD had thrived since its inception. In areas of specialized medical, industrial, financial and other services, Spokane had also established a strong relationship with many Montana and northern Idaho communities.

To emphasize its desire to become an active part of the Spokane business community, DAD leased space in the Old City Hall Building in the heart of the downtown business district. Located on the renowned Spokane skywalk system overlooking Riverfront Park, the site of the 1974 World's Fair, it is one of the most prestigious addresses in the city. Robert L. Cummings was tapped to head the new operation. Bob was a seasoned veteran of the securities business and had filled similar positions with both Kidder Peabody & Co. and with E.F. Hutton. At the opening, he was joined by three experienced Financial Consultants and a back-office manager

Robert Cummings

Dave Milbrath

with more than ten years of seasoning in securities operations. The Spokane move signaled the start of a period of frantic activity which was to run through 1994.

In Spokane, two additional Financial Consultants were added in 1992, and two in 1993. One was Dave Milbrath, one of the best known stockbrokers in eastern Washington. In addition, three professionals joined a burgeoning municipal banking unit under the direction of the Capital Markets Division. They were head-quartered in the Spokane Branch Office where they serviced a growing municipal bond business in western Washington and northern Idaho.

One of the major concerns of DADCO management when it moved into large urban areas was its ability to retain its unique personal relationship with its customers which had become its trademark. While Spokane was not such a large metropolis that it had completely lost its small town flavor, it soon became apparent that this personal relationship could be severely diluted in even a modest-sized community. To aid in maintaining this dimension of its culture, a satellite office of the Spokane Branch was established in the Spokane Valley to serve a growing population in the Post Falls–Coeur d'Alene corridor. A registered Financial Consultant new to DAD, and one already well-established from the Spokane Branch, were chosen to staff the satellite, along with a Registered Associate. Bob Cummings was responsible for its operation, but modern technology provided the staff and its customers with the same information and data as those in the main branch. Satellite offices have enabled DAD to maintain the personal touch with DAD customers which have proved so valuable in other places without incurring the costs associated with establishing another full-fledged office. The customer could drop in and chat with a real live broker and did not have to converse in a one-way conversation with a machine.

By the end of 1994, the Spokane Branch had taken its place as a production leader among all DAD branch offices with ten Financial Consultants assisted by four Registered Associates. It was also poised on the brink of a personnel explosion which would propel it into the top spot.

At the same time, DADCO was moving ahead on several other significant fronts. In September 1992, it announced the completion of the acquisition of American West Tour and Travel, a travel agency located in the Davidson Building. It was DADCO's fourth wholly-owned subsidiary. The new firm was immediately renamed DADCO TRAVEL and opened with an experienced staff of five travel professionals. Darrell Block, DADCO Controller, was named acting President in charge of the operation.

Bruce Madsen returned from his self-imposed "sabbatical" in October 1992 to rejoin DADCO as Vice Chairman. He replaced Gene Hufford who announced his plans to retire after 25 years of distinguished service. In his new position, Bruce was responsible for the overall supervision and coordination of the activities of Financial Aims, TrustCorp, Research

Ray Wooldridge

and the DAD Specialist Posts. One of his first accomplishments was to recruit Fred Dickson as Research Director.

Early in 1993, the firm commenced its fifth Strategic Plan revision. Among other changes, the new plan recommended the expansion of the Board of Directors with the addition of a director outside the company. Raymond E. Wooldridge, President and CEO of Southwest Securities of Dallas, Texas was elected DADCO's first outside director in September 1993 and has made a significant contribution since. Ray served with Ian Davidson on the NASD Board of Governors and is widely known and respected throughout the securities industry.

Michael Morrison, an experienced travel agency executive from Austin, Texas joined DADCO TRAVEL in November as its permanent President. The same month a new branch office was opened in Hamilton, Montana to serve the Bitterroot Valley which had enjoyed an explosive growth. Jim Moerkerke, a DAD Vice President in Missoula, was selected to manage the new

Michael Morrison

office. He was joined by a seasoned Financial Consultant from Spokane and by a Registered Associate who served as office cashier.

Early in 1994, the state granted trust powers to TrustCorp to establish an independent trust company in Washington. In 1989, TrustCorp became the first foreign state granted trust powers to do business in the

State of Idaho. With Washington granting similar powers in 1994, TrustCorp extended its ability to do business in three states. The following July, a second Washington branch office opened in Wenatchee. Rob Johnson was named Vice President and Manager. An experienced Financial Consultant and Registered Associate completed its initial staff.

Finally, the second major urban branch—and DAD's seventeenth— opened in Boise, Idaho on November 4, 1994. Its initial staff consisted of four Financial Consultants and a Registered Associate, with Tom Zemlicka, a 20-year veteran formerly with Piper Jaffray, serving as Manager, and a Registered Associate who headed the support staff. It has since grown to include twelve professionals and a support staff of four, and has become well established in the Boise business community.

By this time, DAD had successfully established new branch offices in two major urban centers. True, neither Spokane nor Boise was in the same class as a Portland, Seattle or Salt Lake City in size or urban sophistication. But they were far larger than any of the major centers heretofore developed in Montana, Wyoming and northern Idaho. Yet the same standards, techniques, and culture employed in developing the smaller communities had been used in Spokane and Boise with equal success.

The success of the DADCO way to expand was reflected in the results chalked up during its initial expansion. Over the three-year period from 1992 to 1995, assets under management grew by more than 81%. The number of DADCO employees had increased by almost 60%, and the firm's capital base increased by over 50%. It seemed that most of the concerns about DAD's ability to compete in the big markets as well as in the small had been successfully addressed. The future for the firm never looked brighter—and it looked as if nothing could stop it.

Then, out of the blue (literally) tragedy struck! In a flash, all the hopes and dreams, which yesterday had seemingly been all but realized, now lay in a pile of rubble at International Airport in Great Falls.

DADCO was again at a crossroads, challenged again by circumstances beyond its control in much the same manner as was Dave Davidson by the backlash of the Great Depression in 1935, and Ian Davidson by the social and cultural revolution of the 1960's.

Again, it was a time of testing.

Out of the Ashes

November 8, 1994, was a beautiful autumn day—the kind that poets drool over and songsters write ballads about. The cloudless skies and crisp cool breezes prompted newscasters to predict a record voter turnout for the day's mid-term election.

The DADCO plane had come in from Idaho the night before after a flawless flight. It had undergone one of its routine detailed inspections a short time before and had performed without a hitch. The scheduled trip to eastern Montana seemed just another routine flight; no different in any way from dozens of others it had made in the years DADCO had owned it.

Only the inevitable brisk autumn breeze was a reminder that it was still November in Montana.

Harry Graf was the pilot assigned to the flight. The firm contracted with Holman Aviation Company for pilots for their authorized flights, and Harry was one of three who were regularly assigned to DADCO. He was an experienced pilot with thousands of total flying hours and had flown the DADCO Beechcraft Baron many, many times. Those who had flown with him were impressed with his skill, his conservatism, and his professionalism. All were comfortable when Harry was at the controls.

So there was no hint of pending doom when Bob Bragg, Gene Lewis and Don Knutson boarded the plane that fateful morning for a trip to Sidney in the far east-central part of Montana. Bob and Gene were slated to conduct one of their popular estate planning seminars which had been arranged by a Sidney tax attorney. Don was to meet with some of his trust company clients in the area. All three planned to return to Great Falls together later that evening.

It was not to be. At a little past ten o'clock that Tuesday morning,

Donald L. (Don) Knutson, 49, was a Senior Vice President and Trust Officer of TrustCorp and TrustCorp Washington. He joined TrustCorp in 1973, and remained upon acquisition by DADCO in 1986. He was the company's lead Trust Officer, bringing in more than a third of total trust assets. Previously, he taught and coached at high schools in Great Falls and Choteau, Montana. Born in Great Falls, Don was a graduate of Concordia College (Moorhead, Minnesota) and the Pacific Coast Banking School. He is survived by his wife, Joanne, and three sons, Jeff, Jon, and Josh.

Robert B. (Bob) Braig, 54, was President and Chief Executive Officers of TrustCorp and TrustCorp Washington, and a Director of DADCO. He joined TrustCorp in 1986, increasing trust assets under management from $85 million to $360 million during his tenure. Previously, he directed a Missoula-based financial and accounting firm, and taught taxation and accounting at the University of Montana School of Business. Born in Terry, Montana, Bob held a B.A. degree from the University of Montana, and was a Certified Public Accountant, Certified Financial Planner, and Certified Business Appraiser. He is survived by his companion, Diana Stefes, and three children, Mike, Marc, and Malina.

Eugene P. (Gene) Lewis, 46, was President and Chief Executive Officer of Financial Aims Corporation, and a Director of DADCO, TrustCorp, and Financial Aims. He joined Financial Aims as Marketing Director in 1989, and was named President later the same year, increasing assets under management from $50 million to $260 million during his tenure. Previously, he held management positions with Entech, Inc., Western Energy Company, and Montana Power Company. Born in Polson, Montana, Gene held B.S. and M.S. degrees from Montana State University–Bozeman. He is survived by his wife, Nancy, and two children, Gena and Max.

after a seemingly routine takeoff, the plane suddenly veered sharply to the left, lost altitude, and crashed, disintegrating into a pile of fiery rubble. All aboard died instantly. Investigation by the Federal Aviation Administration failed to turn up any mechanical failure which would have caused it to malfunction. Ground observers reported that as the plane was taking off, a suit bag belonging to one of the passengers flew out of, or off, the plane and fell to the ground. Whether it had been left on the outside when loading, or whether a storage compartment door had not been secured and came open on takeoff, was a subject of media speculation. The only report on which all observers seemed to agree was that the pilot had apparently reversed his course and was trying to return to the airport when the plane veered out of control and crashed.

The official conclusion called it pilot error. In aviation parlance, this is often a buzz-word for "we don't really know what happened."

The results, however, were disastrous for DADCO.

Bob Bragg was the consummate professional—intense, hard-driving, with a burning desire to be the best at whatever he did. His passion for perfection, however, masked a deeply caring concern for his family, his customers, and his business associates. He was a handsome man with a warm and friendly personality whose presence stood out in any group of which he was a part. In 1963, upon his graduation with a degree in Accounting from the University of Montana, he joined the newly-established D.A. Davidson office in Missoula as a broker. However, after successfully sitting for his CPA designation, he left the securities business to open an accounting practice in Missoula and to teach part-time at the University of Montana as an Adjunct Professor of Accounting.

He became active in the affairs of his profession; and at the time he was elected president of the Montana Society of CPA, he was the youngest person ever to have headed this prestigious organization. His major interest in his field was estate planning and his desire for perfection drove him to take special courses which led to his designation as a specialist in that area.

Ian Davidson and the DAD people in Missoula had maintained a close relationship with Bob after he left the firm; so, when DADCO needed a well-qualified person to head its newly-acquired trust company in 1986, Robert B. Bragg was a strong choice. It was a great fit. He reorganized its administrative structure, added new people and reassigned old ones, and re-energized the entire operation. Within a year he had turned it around from a company whose customer assets it managed were steadily declining to one showing steady growth. At the time of the accident, the trust assets it managed for its customers had grown almost three-and-a-half fold from the time DADCO bought it. Its services had been expanded to five locations in three states. It had the added distinction of having been the first trust company domiciled outside the State of Idaho to become qualified to do business in that state under its unique trust laws.

In spite of the demands on his time required by the business, Bob still continued his commitment to his community and his state. At the time of the crash, he was serving as a Director of DADCO and each of its subsidiaries, TrustCorp and Financial Aims. He was also a director of Great Falls Rotary, the Great Falls Symphony Association, the Montana Ambassadors, and on the Advisory Council of the University of Great Falls. A few months prior to the fatal accident, he had been named by the Montana Ambassadors as its 1994 Ambassador of the Year. He had also occupied virtually every position of leadership in the accounting field in Montana and, in 1981, was named Montana CPA of the Year.

Bob and his wife were divorced, but he remained very close to his three children, Mike, Marc and Malina. He kept the office fully updated on their activities—especially those of Marc who was a Bobcat tight end at Montana State and its star punter. He was justly proud of all his children and their outstanding achievements.

Gene Lewis was a big man in every way—befitting the great Bobcat athlete he had been at Montana State. After earning both a bachelor's and master's degree in Economics from MSU, he taught at the University of Wyoming before joining the Montana Power Company as Director of Resource Planning and Forecasting. In 1984 he entered the securities business as an investment executive with DAD in its Butte office, but returned to Montana Power a year later as Manager of Business Development and Acquisition for two of its subsidiaries. In 1988, he rejoined DADCO as Marketing Manager of Financial Aims Corporation in anticipation of the pending retirement of Bill Macfadden. In 1990 he became President and Chief Executive Officer of Financial Aims.

Under his aggressive leadership, customer assets managed by Financial Aims soared. At the time of his death, it managed more than four times as much in customer assets as it did when he took over. He and Bob Bragg had also developed great synergy between their two DADCO subsidiaries. As a team, they became a very popular feature at financial seminars all over the DADCO region. They were headed to one such event the morning of the plane crash.

At the time of his death, Gene was Chairman of the Montana Council for Economic Education, a member of the Advisory Board of the MSU–Billings College of Business, the Montana Ambassadors, and Vice Chairman of the Governor's Trade Advisory Council.

Gene Lewis was survived by his wife, Nancy, an MSU graduate and a CPA, who was office manager for the Ford dealership in Great Falls; and by their two children, daughter, Gena, married and living in Wyoming; and son, Max, then a student at Carroll College in Helena.

Don Knutson's youthful and choirboy look and demeanor belied his professional competence. As the sports editor of the *Great Falls Tribune* said of Don in a tribute written after the crash, "You would never guess Knutson was a financial whiz or a former star athlete. He didn't look the part, he didn't talk the part, he didn't live the part." Yet, if there is such a thing as an indispensable person in any business, Don Knutson would certainly have been a candidate for that distinction at TrustCorp. He first joined the Trust Company of Montana in 1973 and came to DADCO in 1986 as Vice President and Trust Officer in the transaction which bought the two firms together. He was one of the major assets which triggered interest in the acquisition in the first place. He was responsible for bringing to TrustCorp more than one-third of the $360 million of assets it managed at the time of his death.

Born in Havre, Montana, Don was raised in Great Falls where he was an outstanding athlete and student. At Great Falls High School, he earned all-state honors in 1962 as a member of its state championship basketball team. He went on to star at Concordia College in Moorhead, Minnesota as a four-year basketball starter. He returned to Montana to coach and teach at Choteau and Great Falls before joining Trust Company of Montana in 1973.

Don was a graduate of the Pacific Coast Banking School, and an outstanding golfer. But above all, he was a consummate family man. He and his wife, Joanne, also a top-flight golfer, have three sons, Jeff, Jon and Josh. Jeff starred in football at Concordia; while Jon, one of Montana's most outstanding high school athletes, was a highly recruited football lineman at the University of Colorado. Josh was still in high school when his Dad died. Don was a leader in Boy Scouts, the Civitan Club, and Meadow Lark Country Club. He was also a lay leader in his

Lutheran Church.

In the life of almost every person there is some event which happens or some revelation that occurs which seems to define his or her *raison d' être*. The same is true for an institution. The 1994 plane crash was such an event at DADCO.

The morning of November 8, 1994, is still etched vividly in my memory. I came into the building by a back door leading to the lot where I parked my car. The building was off-limits to smokers, and the backdoor entry was a favorite hangout for those who had not yet kicked the habit. Jim Searles was quietly smoking; his demeanor pensive and grim. I gave him some sort of flippant greeting which failed to elicit the usual repartee. Instead, he quietly asked, "Have you heard the news?" His tone warned me that it was not good.

"No, what?"

"The company plane crashed a few moments ago. There are no survivors."

I knew Bob, Gene and Don were scheduled for a trip to eastern Montana. But it could not be! I had just had lunch the noon before with Don and he was to leave Friday for Boulder for the weekend to watch Jon and his Colorado Buffaloes play Notre Dame.

In a trance, I made my way to the second floor. It could well have been a morgue. People were at their desks going through the motions, but a cloud of disbelief and incredulity hung heavily over each.

Ian was in conference when the news came in. Business immediately came to a crashing halt. After a few moments to let the awful reality sink in, he huddled with his key managers, and together they arranged to break the news to Nancy Lewis, Joanne Knutson, Diane Steffes, Bob Bragg's special friend, and Karen Graf in personal visits. It was, he said later, the hardest thing he had ever had to do.

The local noon news was devoted almost entirely to the details of the tragedy. By then, the national media had picked up the story—and the phones began to ring. The response was overwhelming, reflecting the stature of the victims and the impact of their contributions on their community and their state. It was also a testimonial to the high regard in which the Davidson organization was held in the Montana business community.

Messages of condolence and offers of assistance poured in, many from unexpected sources. A local automobile dealer called to say that he was arranging for up to seven vans to be available for the use of family members of the victims, or for out-of-town employees in to pay their respects to the families. An airline executive offered free flights for relatives to Great Falls and return. The pastor of the church where many of the Davidson family—including D.A. Davidson—had worshipped came by to offer counseling services, as well as help in funeral arrangements. A professional grief counselor called to say that he was available to conduct sessions for both family members and any employees who felt a need, all without charge.

The managers of two competing securities firms offered people to handle phone calls during the memorial and funeral services for each of the victims. The high school which the Knutson boys attended offered the use of its auditorium for a public memorial service for the victims, and the symphonic choir of which Jon Knutson had been a part in high school, would provide music if desired.

These were only a few of the scores of expressions of shock, grief, and offers to help with which the firm and the families were inundated during the days immediately following the crash. It was a ringing endorsement of the essential goodness of the human spirit which was so much a part of the faith of the Davidson heritage as passed down from George Davidson to those who followed.

Despite a sense of overwhelming personal loss, some urgent business decisions had to be made. On Friday, about 300 out-of-town people were slated to arrive for the DADCO Annual Meeting. Speakers had been invited, rooms reserved, and arrangements made. All had to be changed or canceled. The annual meeting of the NASD Board of Governors was scheduled to meet in Washington, D.C. the following week. Ian Davidson was to be elected its Chairman—the highest non-administrative post in the securities industry.

These events, important though they were, were secondary to the needs of the families of the victims, and those of the friends and business associates of the three friends suddenly cut down in the prime of their lives. The DADCO meeting was canceled, and Ian missed his first and only meeting during his three-year tenure on the NASD Board of Governors. However, not only was he elected Chairman, but the Board issued a Memorial Resolution extolling the contributions of Bob Bragg, Gene Lewis, and Don Knutson to the securities industry. The Board of Governors subsequently made a $20,000 contribution to the Bragg/Lewis/Knutson Memorial Scholarship Fund established to permanently memorialize the efforts of the three executives to advance the cause of economic education.

The Scholarship Fund is used to provide grants to eligible DADCO employees to assist them to further their education at an institution of higher education of their choice. Their field of study need not be related to their job, or even to the securities industry. It has already provided help for almost two dozen employees in the time it has been in existence.

In the ensuing weeks, tributes still continued to come in. Dennis Washington, a prominent Missoula industrialist, established nine college scholarships in honor of the three executives; and the Montana Ambassadors memorialized their contributions to the Montana business community in a Memorial Resolution.

In 1995, DADCO set up the Bragg/Lewis/Knutson Community Service Award given annually to the company employee who best exemplifies the ideal of community service through his or her contributions to their community. The name of the recipient is permanently displayed on a plaque in the lobby of the Davidson Building, with a smaller replica presented to the recipient at the DADCO Annual Meeting. The firm also makes a donation to a charity selected by the recipient in his or her honor.

It has become the firm's most prestigious and coveted honor.

The balance of the week following the crash still remains a blur. Small groups of employees met repeatedly with Dr. Bill Taylor, a skilled crisis counselor. In several departments, people met spontaneously in prayer and discussion sessions in an effort to work their way though their shock and grief to some sort of inner peace. Not only had each of the three victims been a key leader in some phase of the firm's operation, but each was a personal friend to almost everyone in DADCO and their passing left a huge void in a great number of lives. It took time to adjust to the suddenness and the finality of what had happened.

On Thursday evening, DADCO said its own good-bye in a memorial service in the Bill Williamson Auditorium at C.M. Russell High School. Hundreds of employees and friends from all parts of the state and beyond jammed the hall. Grahame Nicolson, pastor of a community church in Conrad, presented the spiritual assurances, while members of the DADCO family remembered Bob and Gene and Don with touching eulogies. Nicolson was a former DAD Investment Executive in Havre. He had been ordained as a minister in his native Australia before emigrating to the United States. He had a successful career with DAD, but the call to the ministry was strong in him, and when the opportunity arose to serve a small community church in Conrad, he felt compelled to forsake a successful securities career for his first love. He still remains a warm friend of DAD and its people.

Separate funeral services for Bob Bragg and Gene Lewis were conducted on Friday, both from the Congregational Church. The Reverend Jim Peterson presided at each service before a standing-room only crowd. Hundreds more jammed the Faith Lutheran Church on Saturday morning where farewells were said to Don Knutson; while a final good-bye was bid Harry Graf, the pilot, in a somewhat smaller service at a local mortuary on Saturday afternoon.

In all, more than 2,000 people are estimated to have attended one or more of the four services honoring those who lost their lives on that fatal Tuesday morning. The Davidson plane crash altered the future plans of a host of local and state organizations and its repercussions extended even to a national level. But no where were they felt so profoundly as at DADCO. While each of the dead executives had played an important role in shaping the programs of the community and educational groups with whom they had been actively involved, at DADCO each was a key figure in the future success of a particular area of the business which he headed. It was as though each had been a star quarterback of a team vying for the league championship. The loss threw each into a state of chaos. Had DADCO been a stock which was publicly traded, the sudden death of three of its key decision-makers would have unquestionably caused a precipitous drop in its price.

But, as so often happens when a well-coached team suffers a disastrous loss, tragedy defined its character. Like the phoenix of fable, there arose from the ashes of disaster a closing of the ranks, a heightened sense of purpose, and an increased effort on the part of each person in each department which was directly affected by the loss.

More than any other single event, the outpouring of goodwill on the part of the community, the added effort which each co-worker dedicated to his or her job, and the tributes to the character and contribution of each who lost his life helped to define the DADCO culture—those qualities which give each organization its unique character and sets it apart from its peers, each with its own distinctive personality. It has established for Bob Bragg, Don Knutson and Gene Lewis a permanent place of honor in the annals of the firm as examples of the best there is in the DADCO culture. It insures the immortality of their memories for all the years to come.

Community Service

*Chuck McAdam with his
Special Olympians.*

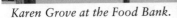

Karen Grove at the Food Bank.

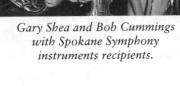

*Gary Shea and Bob Cummings
with Spokane Symphony
instruments recipients.*

*Tom, Ken, Doug, and Stu Nicholson —
all Eagle Scouts.*

To date, there have been six recipients of the
Bragg/Lewis/Knutson Community Service Award.

Ken Reesman – 1995

Chuck McAdam – 1996

Cort Wilcox – 1997

Stu Nicholson – 1998

Karen Grove – 1999

Page Dabney – 2000

Regrouping

The outpouring of public support and goodwill and the added dedication and effort put forth by each affected DADCO employee did much to soften the impact of the sudden loss of three key executives in the 1994 plane crash. But it did not alter the reality that a serious disruption had occurred in DADCO's plans for the future. Management was confronted with some important new decisions.

The Company's entry into major urban markets in Spokane and Boise had gone more smoothly than even DAD had hoped. This success had begun to generate a great deal of enthusiasm and momentum for the future. The tragedy abruptly dampened both; and uncertainty arose as to how it would affect the firm's future expansion plans. There are constantly recurring personnel shifts and new job assignments which come naturally as a firm grows and expands. But the loss of the kind of leadership which DADCO had suffered raised some serious questions about the ability of the company to withstand the loss and still move forward with its ambitious agenda for the future. Three of those normal personnel shifts were particularly awkward, coming as they did so soon after the crash.

Bob Retz announced his intention to step down as Director or Retail Branches by year's end. When he joined DAD, he had committed himself to the firm for five years, after which he had indicated that he intended to seriously consider retirement. He was deeply involved with his sons in a recreational real estate development in the Flathead Valley which needed his guidance. It was pure coincidence that Bob's decision to retire followed so closely on the heels of the crash. It was something that had been pre-planned and there was no connection between them; but it did leave one more hole to fill in the DADCO leadership on top of those caused by the crash. Also, negotiations that had started before the crash between the chief economic strategist at Financial Aims and a West Coast investment group were finalized soon after the crash. He resigned to accept the new position. This created a double void. His companion was a trust officer at TrustCorp and she elected to move with him when he left. The result was major vacancies in three key positions in addition to those created by the tragedy.

Also, Ian Davidson had just been elected the new Chairman of the Board of the NASD Board of Governors, one of the most prestigious honors in the entire securities industry. Though the recognition was invaluable to enhance the national stature of the firm, it entailed "hands on" management on Ian's part which would require a huge commitment of his time away from DADCO during his term. It was with considerable trepidation that he somewhat reluctantly agreed to accept the honor and the commitment it entailed.

It was at this point that the character, quality and commitment of the management team which he had so carefully assembled proved its worth. Douglas Blattmachr was lured back west from a specialty money management firm in his native New York to head TrustCorp. Doug had spent nearly twenty years in the trust business in Alaska and Idaho before returning east to head a $30 billion firm with 700 employees. The laid-back western lifestyle was hard to resist, however, and when the call from DADCO came, it was too appealing to ignore.

Financial Aims looked within for solutions. Soon after the crash, Jack Davant was named its Chief Operating Officer. Jack was a 20-year veteran with DAD, starting as an Account Executive in Bozeman in 1977, and joining FAC as a Portfolio Manager in 1981. He was Senior Vice President and Portfolio Manager at the time of Gene Lewis' death. In recognition of his contributions as COO, the Board chose Jack as President of Financial Aims at its mid-year meeting in June; and he was elected a Director of DADCO at the annual shareholders meeting in December.

One of Jack's first acts was to recruit Bruce Morison as Senior Portfolio Manager. Morison brought to FAC an impressive record in asset management and security analysis in both the banking and mutual fund fields. At the same time, Brad Houle, who had been associated with an Oregon securities firm since completing the DAD investment executive training program as an intern in 1990, joined FAC as Portfolio Coordinator. (Score another payoff for the Intern Training Program.)

As a result of their prompt reorganization, and the dedicated performance in each company, neither Financial Aims nor TrustCorp missed a beat during the period of adjustment. Assets under management during the period increased 20% at Financial Aims and 30% at TrustCorp. Shortly after Blattmachr's arrival, an experienced trust office from the Norwest Bank organization joined TrustCorp to replace Anne Sanders who left with him when Bob Anton resigned from FAC.

Finding a successor to Bob Retz took a bit longer. Since the next major step on the DADCO expansion agenda anticipated a move into the Seattle–Portland area, it was important to have someone with strong ties to that area as a Director of Retail Branches. An intensive search culminated in the choice of Paul Wonnacott. It was a happy one. Paul brought to DAD a record of more than 25 years of outstanding success. He started his career in Toronto with a Canadian firm, but for the past fifteen years had managed some of the most successful branch office operations on the Pacific Coast for some of the largest securities firms in the business. His most recent assignment had been with Merrill Lynch where he supervised a force which included more than 80 financial consultants and their support staff. He had also managed similar organizations for Prudential Securities, E. F. Hutton and Drexel-Burnham.

A number of his changes in company affiliations had been triggered by mergers and takeovers which are becoming increasingly common in all business. It created a sense of uncertainty about the future, not only for Paul, but for the customers and employees as well. When DAD approached Paul with an opportunity to acquire a personal ownership in a firm in which he could, to some extent, dictate his own future, it was very appealing; particularly when the firm was privately owned by its employees and had a capital base strong enough to finance its future expansion out of its own resources. Add to that a culture that prided itself on building strong personal relationships with its customers, its employees and the communities it served and it became an irresistible opportunity for a Paul Wonnacott. It has proved to be one of the strongest attractions DAD has to offer as it moves into the major markets of the Pacific Northwest. This personal touch has served it well thus far, and

Gerry Meyer

bodes well for the future as the story unfolds.

The team approach developed between Vinney Purpura, Gerry Meyer and Bob Retz also appealed to Paul Wonnacott. While each member had his own sphere of expertise within the team, all were committed to the common goal of establishing and staffing successful branch offices in appropriate locations throughout the Pacific Northwest and Northern Rocky Mountain region which were dedicated to the principles of the DADCO culture. It was the basic blueprint which had been successful in establishing offices in Spokane and Boise. With some refinements, it held great promise for the future in the more populous areas.

1995 and much of 1996 were years of regrouping, filling holes, and consolidating gains already made. Ian Davidson spent much of 1995 on NASD work as Chairman of its Board of Governors. It turned out to be one of the most significant years which the National Association of Securities Dealers had experienced since it was established in 1938. For several years prior to 1995, the NASD and its wholly-owned electronic trading market, NASDAQ, had been under pressure from Arthur Levitt, SEC Chairman, and some key committees of Congress for alleged irregularities on the part of some NASD members, as well as conflicts of interest. While in 1995 only three firms in a thousand and one individual in a thousand engaged in any kind of unethical practice sufficiently grave to warrant a temporary suspension or a permanent expulsion from the business, there was sufficient perception that the opportunity existed for wrongdoing to warrant making some major changes. Like Caesar's wife, the industry was held to a higher standard, and in an ever-increasingly skeptical society, even the perception that the system might lend itself to abuse was reason enough for it to carefully re-examine its structure and safeguards to protect the investor. For several years the Board had wrestled with the problem. As a self-regulatory body, the NASD had the duty to protect investors and to investigate and adjudicate complaints brought against NASD members or against NASDAQ, the electronic trading market it owned and operated.

The results of months of discussions and research came to a head on Ian Davidson's watch. As a result, unprecedented changes, the most profound since the NASD was established, were made during his year of leadership. Following the recommendations of a Select Committee headed by former Senator Warren Rudman, responsibility for the operation of the NASDAQ market was separated from the regulation of the nation's broker/dealers. Two distinct companies were formed which, while related, operated separately from each other. Each was governed by its own Board of Directors and each had significant public representation in its governing structure. NASD Regulations, Inc. oversees the activities of more than 505,000 registered professionals in 58,000 branch offices in 5,400 firms. It also oversees the markets operated by its sister subsidiary, the NASDAQ Stock Market, Inc. Each company will have at least 50% representation on its Board from outside the securities industry. A strengthened Office of Internal Review conducts internal audits of NASD Regulation, Inc. and acts as an ombudsman for regulatory or market concerns. A new Office of Investor Services will monitor and advance the views of individual investors.

In 1995, the NASD and NASDAQ Boards acted decisively to expand investor opportunities for price improvement in buying or selling securities on NASDAQ. They also approved structural changes which expanded NASDAQ's capacity to handle one billion shares a day; and strengthened the NASD regulatory resources by approving an 18% increase in its 1996 budget for regulation and related technology support.

In total, 1995 was a remarkable year for the NASD — a tribute to Ian Davidson's decisive leadership, the same kind that he had been giving to DADCO and its predecessors for more than a quarter of a century.

Back at home, things continued to hum. DADCO acquired a new plane to replace the one destroyed in the crash. Despite the safety questions raised after it went down, management early on made a decision that a company plane was the only practical answer to the Company's extensive travel needs. It commissioned an independent firm which specialized in corporate aviation to do an in-depth study of its air transportation requirements. As a result, a five-passenger plus two pilots Piper Cheyenne twin turbo prop was selected, and Dan Johannes, a veteran pilot and aircraft maintenance technician, was hired as a full-time Director of Flight Services. He was backed up by a full-time company co-pilot. These new appointments followed a recommendation that the operators of all DADCO aircraft be company employees.

The new plane was immediately put to work. Some extensive and intensive negotiations brought a specialized Spokane investment group to DAD. The thirteen-person Investment Planning Group, headed by R.C. Roland and Garry Shea, had developed a sophisticated portfolio analysis system offered to clients on a fee-for-service basis. DAD provides trade execution, record-storing and retrieval, performance reporting, and other services for a fixed charge. It also allowed IPG to offer money

R.C. Roland   Garry Shea

management services to clients at a very controlled cost.

It also required DAD to modify its record keeping and other services to accommodate the needs of IPG. Again the innovative skills of Vinney Purpura and his staff came to the fore. The changes were made and IPG has become a major contributor to the success of D.A. Davidson & Co. in the Spokane area.

At the same time that the Investment Planning Group was settling in with DAD on what was then the western edge of its active territory, a major expansion was taking place in Billings on the east. Gary Buchanan, one of the most respected figures in Montana's securities industry, joined D.A. Davidson & Co. as a Senior Vice President, Institutional Sales in the Magic City. Gary had a long and illustrious career in both business and public service. Entering the securities business in 1979 with Merrill Lynch, he had held major management positions with both Merrill Lynch and Dain Bosworth. In 1980, he interrupted his business career to become Montana's first Director of its newly-created Department of Commerce. Later he served as Chairman of the Montana Banking Board and on the Montana Trade Commission. A long list of volunteer organizations in which he and his wife, Norma, have long been active include United Way, Easter Seal, and the Mental Health Association.

Joining in his move to DAD was Janice Cochrane, his long-time Executive Assistant who had been with Gary since his days at the Department of Commerce. She is a registered professional in her own right.

Gary Buchanan

The satellite system, already successfully tested in the Spokane Valley area was extended. New satellites were established in Sandpoint and Moscow-Pullman in Idaho, and in Miles City and Livingston in Montana. In addition, banks in Helena and Great Falls established satellites within their institutions to provide brokerage services to their customers without requiring them to build and train a staff to provide the necessary ongoing service.

As 1996 drew to a close, DADCO was ready to make its move. Ian Davidson's term on both the NASD and Pacific Exchange Boards had expired. On the latter, Bruce Madsen had replaced him to assure that the Company would continue to play an active role in PCX affairs. The firm's data retrieval and other communication systems had been updated and a highly trained staff was in place to assure that those who used them were able to get the information they needed when they needed it.

A new position of Chief Investment Officer had been created and Randy Yoakum, a Chartered Financial Advisor with an impressive record of accomplishment in supervising the activities of equity traders and portfolio managers who direct the investment of customer assets, had been chosen to fill it. His job was to coordinate the investment decisions between Financial Aims, Davidson Trust, and the Research Department to maximize investment results in all areas of DADCO to the extent possible within the limitations of its conservative parameters.

DAD had successfully established itself in Spokane and Boise; had regrouped from the disruptions caused by the plane crash; and was positioned for the challenges awaiting it as it set out to storm the bastions of Seattle, Portland and Salt Lake City — and complete its goal to become the premier securities firm in the Northern Rocky Mountains and Pacific Northwest.

Westward Ho!

A properly-crafted story is supposed to start at the beginning and follow a neat, orderly chronological path to a logical conclusion. We have tried to be true to this basic rule. But being a simple—and at times illogical—human being, we are often unable to grasp the significance of events at the time they occur and put them in their proper sequence. We often fail to make the connection between actions taken at a given point in time and their effect on future results. As a result, our story may seem at times to come across more disjointed than a well-crafted story should. This is particularly true when the author tries to relate to happenings while they are still unfolding.

Sometimes, too, we interrupt the chronological flow of events to set some groundwork in order to emphasize their significance. Sometimes unforeseen circumstances dictate that we interrupt the customary sequence. A bit of each is involved in describing the development of the urban markets of the Pacific Northwest.

As early as 1985, DADCO formally declared its intention, in its second Strategic Planning Conference, to become the premier securities firm in the Northern Rocky Mountains and Pacific Northwest. All strategic plans since have reconfirmed this goal. No firm could claim such a distinction without having a major presence in the urban metropolitan areas of the region. It went almost without saying that DAD could not realize its goal unless it established major branch offices in Seattle, Portland and Salt Lake City and had strong representation in the smaller surrounding communities which comprised their respective trade areas. Every action taken since 1985 has been with this goal in mind. However, a great deal of preliminary groundwork was necessary before active development could begin. Included among these were:

- To establish Specialist Posts on the Pacific Exchange for the purpose of gaining experience in competing in major urban markets; to gain national exposure and recognition for the firm; and to create another source of revenue which the company would use to finance the cost of other expansion without incurring costly debt.
- Financial planning, asset analysis and management, and insurance services offered through Financial Aims and Davidson Trust were essential if the firm was to successfully compete in urban markets against Wall Street wirehouses with their vast resources and national reputations.
- The firm could not truly become a full-service, diversified financial services organization if it was not able to offer the same kind of investment banking and underwriting services in a regional market as its Wall Street competitors did on a national level.
- Basic to all these services was a research capability which could seek out, analyze, and evaluate financial products which were appropriate for each customer, individual and corporate, and could produce maximum value for each within each individual's comfort level of risk.

To attract customers to DAD and keep them coming back, its Financial Consultants had to have superior training and be dedicated to growing value for their clients. To keep Financial Consultants current in the ever-changing economic and social climate, DAD established a program of continuing education for all employees to ensure that all customers would receive the best service and most up-to-date advice available. It also made extensive and ongoing investments in the latest technology to give each employee the tools to do his or her job with the maximum of accuracy and efficiency.

From its beginning, the selection of stocks, bonds and other financial products recommended to DADCO customers has rested with Financial Consultants, trust officers, and portfolio managers. Each analyst in the Research Department follows the fundamental and technical trends that historically affect the price fluctuations of a relatively small number of individual stocks. From their research, they make recommendations to those dealing directly with customers as to which should be bought or sold to satisfy a particular financial need for a given situation.

To improve its competitive position, it also became apparent that there was a need to consolidate all investment decisions, then made separately by trust officers, portfolio managers and research analysts, in one place where they could be coordinated and accountability could be pinpointed. It was confusing to customers to have a stock strongly recommended by one part of the company and shunned by another. It tended to weaken confidence in the quality of all DAD research. To avoid such confusion and inconsistencies, the Board created a new executive position of Chief Investment Officer.

Early in 1997, DADCO was ready to intensify its move to the west and south. The groundwork for it had, in reality, started with the hiring of a Chief Investment Officer, and Paul Wonnacott as Director of Retail Branches in 1995. Paul's prominence and prestige in the Seattle–Portland area had played a vital role in his choice. Immediately after joining DAD, he and Gerry Meyer began to screen potential candidates to fill positions to be created when the firm started to staff new offices as they opened. From that point on, activity accelerated at breakneck speed. In late February, Paul Wonnacott and Gerry Meyer scored their first major success of the western expansion with the appointment of Bob Magnuson as Western Regional Director of Retail Branches. Bob's immediate assignment was the development of the Seattle area for D.A. Davidson & Co.

Bob Magnuson

A veteran of more than 20 years in the securities industry, Bob Magnuson had joined Piper Jaffray in Minneapolis immediately after graduation from college. In 1983, PJH asked him to move to Seattle where he was charged with developing a Pacific Northwest District for his firm. Under his leadership, the District grew into one of the major operations, not only in PJH, but among all companies doing business on the Pacific Coast.

The wave of mergers between giants in the financial services industry had caused many of their employees to be uneasy about the future direction their new organization would take. Bobby Piper, the chief engineer of the growth at PJH, was a friend, and had been something of a role model for Ian Davidson. They shared many of the same values with regard to their business culture. Bob Magnuson, a protégé of

Seattle Office.

Bobby Piper, had grown up in a business culture similar to that at DADCO. So he was very comfortable with the environment he found at his new firm.

It is an environment which was to prove to be one of DADCO's major assets in attracting quality people for its westward expansion.

Had the usual sequence of development been strictly observed, the company would have given its full attention to the Seattle development until it was up, running, and turning a profit. But again, circumstances intervened. Daren Shaw, a highly successful investment banking professional in Portland, Oregon, indicated a desire to return to his native Utah. Salt Lake City was one of DAD's major targets for expansion. So three weeks after the appointment of Bob Magnuson in Seattle, the Capital Markets Group announced the opening of an investment banking branch in Salt Lake City, and the appointment of Daren Shaw as its Managing Director of Corporate Finance.

It was the first step toward the establishment of a major presence for DADCO in the State of Utah.

While all this was going on, activity was heating up in the trust area. For some time, Doug Blattmachr, President of TrustCorp, together with his brother, a prominent tax and trust attorney in New York, had been at work with officials of an Alaska trust company to shape legislation which would allow trust companies domiciled in Alaska to serve as fiduciaries for foreign asset protection trusts so popular in Switzerland, Cayman Island, and other offshore jurisdictions. Such trusts offered unique tax advantages for corporations and individuals with large estates.

In April, the enabling legislation was approved and a locally-domiciled majority partner was found to join DADCO in a joint venture in the Alaska Trust Company. The law, as approved, required that the majority interest in the venture be owned by Alaska citizens. Doug Blattmachr became President and CEO of Alaska Trust. He moved to Anchorage, where he had previously lived for some ten years, to assume active management of the new joint venture. The name of TrustCorp was changed to Davidson Trust Co. to emphasize its DADCO affiliation and to capitalize on the growing prestige of the Davidson name in the Pacific Northwest. Joe Heffernan joined Davidson Trust in July as Senior Trust Officer and was asked to assume active management of its trust operations pending the appointment of a permanent CEO. Two new experienced trust officers were also added, one in Great Falls and one in Billings, to further strengthen the trust company staff. Blattmachr temporarily retained his position as Chairman of Davidson Trust and a Director of DADCO.

Joe Heffernan

However, as with all of life, the highway was not always smooth and straight. Sometimes there are bumps. Fred Dickson, who, in his brief tenure as Research Director, had built an enviable reputation for his perceptive research and his willingness to share with both customers and Financial Consultants, resigned to accept a position with a firm in Virginia. Fred was a strong family man and a devout churchman. Both his daughters had finished college and had embarked on careers on the east coast. His new job provided him an opportunity to pursue religious studies at a nearby seminary and at the same time be closer to his daughters. So, it was with great reluctance, on the part of both Fred and DAD, that he said "farewell."

The balance of 1997 and the early part of 1998 resembled a three-ring (or more) circus with furious activity going on in several arenas at once. When Daren Shaw opened an investment banking office in February, it was expected to be a prelude to a major retail branch office later. In August, the expectation became a reality. A team of seasoned veterans, Rex Thornton and James Wheeler, joined DAD as Senior Vice Presidents to co-manage the Salt Lake City retail operation. Both were previously associated with Piper Jaffray where they had also worked together. They brought with them three Registered Associates, two of whom had been with them at PJH.

Two months later, the Hansen Group, a unique specialized team consisting of a father and two sons, joined the Salt Lake Branch. Thornton and Wheeler had worked with them at Piper. Ken Hansen, the father and senior member of the group, had entered the securities business with J.A. Hogle & Co. in Salt Lake City in 1962, just four years after Ian Davidson had left that firm to join his father at what was to become D.A. Davidson & Co.

What goes around comes around!

The Salt Lake Branch opened in August in temporary quarters, pending the completion of a new Deseret News Building in downtown Salt Lake City. In February 1998, it celebrated the opening of its new quarters in the newly-completed building with an open house which attracted many business and community leaders. Its location gives D.A. Davidson & Co. one of the most prestigious addresses in the Salt Lake City business community and will provide a prime work environment for 18 to 20 people. By the end of February 1998, the space was nearly half full.

In the same month of August 1997, DADCO was honored by the School of Business of Montana State University as its Family Business of the Year in its Large Company category. The award, now in its fourth year, honors firms who have excelled in their field

Family Business of the Year Plaque.

and have their roots in Montana. The selection was made on the basis of information supplied in a ten-page questionnaire. A clearly enunciated policy on the business ethics actively practiced by the firm, and the promotion of community service on the part of the firm's employees are among the factors which weigh heavily in the final selection.

Also in August, in another ring of its circus, DAD opened its tenth Specialist Post on the Pacific Exchange and its fifth on its Los Angeles Floor— And August is supposed to be a vacation month when everything shuts down and folks are interested only in playing!

The pace continued through the end of the year, and did not let up in 1998. September saw the Capital Investment Advisors join DAD as part of the Boise Branch. This is a group of three professional money managers who guide the investment decisions for individuals and corporations with large portfolios. All three principals had previously been associated with a large bank in Boise which merged with another chain. Again, DADCO's customer-oriented approach and its flexibility to create customized solutions to meet the particular needs of an unconventional situation made DAD attractive to this specialty group. DAD will execute all transactions arising from portfolio changes recommended by the managers.

In the meantime, expansion continued elsewhere. Seattle continued to grow with the addition of an Assistant Manager and several new Financial Consultants. New branch offices were opened in Aberdeen and Redmond, Washington under Bob Magnuson's guidance. Capital Markets established a major presence in the Seattle area with the addition of three well-known professionals in the institutional fixed income sector and one in institutional equity sales. They operate as an arm of the Seattle Branch.

DADCO TRAVEL announced the acquisition of a Missoula travel agency with a professionally-trained staff of five. It was the first expansion of the travel service since its start. New satellites of the Spokane and Bozeman branches became operational, and a Senior Portfolio Manager joined Financial Aims from one of the nation's largest mutual fund organizations.

However, probably the most significant addition to the long-range expansion of DADCO made during this hectic period was its acquisition of Jensen Securities in Portland, Oregon. Jensen is a "boutique" research organization which maintains intensive, high-quality research on more than 85 companies based in the Pacific Northwest. Its clients include some of the nation's largest mutual fund and institutional banking organizations. Its 20 professionals include four senior analysts and a large support staff that publishes hundreds of in-depth reports each year on the companies in their region.

In February 1998, the merger of Jensen into DADCO was completed and Jensen Securities became a detached arm of the Research Department of D.A. Davidson & Co. Its research operations have been melded into the research functions of DADCO where it will continue to specialize in regional research. This entry into the Portland investment community gave DAD the exposure to enable it to establish a full-service retail branch in downtown Portland as its last major building block in its Pacific Northwest structure on September 1. The Portland branch was opened with a nine-person staff headed by Russell W. Tennant as Vice President and Manager, assisted by four veteran Financial Consultants and four support staff assistants.

The rapid expansion of DADCO and its subsidiaries in 1997 and 1998 brought other needs to the fore. Among them was a space crisis in its headquarters building. The addition of new branches and units requiring special handling necessitated more people at all levels, but especially in the operations and clerical services area. Space in the original Davidson Building had been remodeled and reconfigured until there was literally no place to put more people. Ian Davidson had foreseen such a condition when, some years earlier, he purchased the balance of the half-block to the west of the building, which had been cleared of all its existing structures. This provided ample space for expansion when, and if, it became necessary. As early as 1995, when the success of the Spokane venture confirmed DAD's ability to successfully compete in major urban centers, it became apparent that the time was fast approaching when a major expansion of its headquarters facilities would be required.

The first step was taken in 1996 with the purchase of the Liberty Center which we described earlier. But before any space relief could be given to those cramped in the Davidson Building, several important problems had to be addressed. Unrestricted access between the two buildings was essential for the free flow of communication between all departments of the company. This could be accomplished by an overhead skywalk connecting the two buildings at the second floor level. Before that could happen, however, the City of Great Falls had to agree to close off the street to vehicular travel between the two buildings in order to accommodate the necessary supporting tower. The street closure would also eliminate a number of spaces for customer parking, both for DADCO, and other downtown businesses.

It was not until late 1996 that the whole project came together. The City Commission authorized the street closure. A west entrance was added to the Davidson Building. Customer parking in the amphitheatre to the west replaced that lost by the closing of the street. In late 1996, work started on the skywalk, as well as on a major renovation of the first floor of the Liberty Center to accommodate the first of several DADCO departments which would ultimately be relocated.

From that point on, construction proceeded at a rapid rate. On December 4, 1998, the skywalk was opened and along with the Davidson Court on Third Street, dedicated in a public ceremony featuring local civic leaders, as well as Montana's lieutenant-governor and its senior United States senator. The amphitheatre and landscaped parking area to the west of the Davidson Building, known as the Circle Plaza, was completed in early 1999. Much of the space in the Liberty Center has since been remodeled to meet the requirements of the Davidson Trust Company, Accounting and Client Support services, Communication, Compliance, and other departments, now housed there. In total, well over half of the space in the Liberty Center is already, or soon will be, occupied by DADCO people. It will allow room for needed expansion for the Corporate Headquarters staff, Capital Markets, Syndicate, and the remaining DADCO units in the Davidson Building to take place. Much of it has already begun.

Already, also, there is evidence of a resurgence of vitality in the downtown area around the Davidson Court and Circle Plaza. Several new businesses have sprung up, and some existing ones are expanding. While there is no hard evidence that the DADCO project is responsible, the ambience which the Court and Circle provide to the central business district has certainly made the area a more attractive place for people to work and shop.

To that extent, the hope nurtured by Ian Davidson that the expansion of his firm would provide a spark which would ignite action on the part of others to do likewise seems to be taking place.

As the 20th Century passed into history, the firm Dave Davidson had launched in 1935 had just embarked on its 65th year. It had already achieved many of the goals, unspoken, but real, first envisioned by Ian Davidson in his Berkeley thesis in 1956, formalized in the 1985 Strategic

Plan, and reconfirmed in each succeeding revision. It had moved a single three-person retail stock brokerage office in the Steele Building to a 34-office financial services conglomerate employing more than 700 people in six states, offering as wide a variety of financial services as almost any firm of its kind in the nation.

More important, it had achieved its growth while maintaining its distinction as the premier firm of its kind in its region—if not the entire industry. It has become the standard by which others are measured. The quality of any organization cannot be divorced from the quality of the character of the people who make it go. You cannot talk about DADCO without mentioning Ian Davidson. The late Michael P. Malone, President of Montana State University and one of the West's most renowned and respected historians, published Montana: A Contemporary Profile in 1996. In it, Dr. Malone profiles the contributions of some of the businesses and people in Great Falls who have had a significant impact on the development of Montana. Included is the excerpt: "...Great Falls is Montana's major center of state-based companies, including ... D.A. Davidson & Co. Led by CEO Ian Davidson, perhaps the state's most prominent businessman, the company is the largest investment firm in the West, excluding California."

The impact of Ian Davidson and the firm he built extends far beyond the confines of Great Falls itself. In the waning months of the 20th Century, both the *Great Falls Tribune* and the daily *Missoulian* published similar profiles on the 100 Montanans of the Century—those who, in the opinion of the staff that prepared the lists, had had the most profound impact on the state in the last 100 years.

Neither used the same criteria in their selections, nor did their staffs compare notes. In fact, each paper is a part of a different national chain. Ian Davidson was included on both lists. The *Missoulian* attempted to rank their selections in the order of their lasting influences on Montana. Ian was in the top third in their ranking. The *Tribune* made no such distinction, but the reporter who interviewed him for the story told Ian unofficially that he was on a short list of their top 25. Montana is certainly aware of DAD and the Davidsons and what they have contributed to its economy and its culture.

In like manner, both are recognized at a national level. In May, 1998, Forbes published a book by Robert J. Froehlick, whom we mentioned earlier. Bob Froehlick sent Ian a complimentary copy. An inscription on its fly-leaf reads:

"Ian:

I have had the privilege of working with just about every single firm in our industry, no matter the size or location. When someone asks me which firm is the best, I never hesitate to answer: D.A. Davidson & Co. The reason for my answer is you! The success of any firm is determined at the top. You are not only a great leader, but a visionary as well. I am honored to have been given the opportunity to work with you and your Number 1 firm!

Best wishes!

5-6-98"

Bob Froehlick

Ian's response the Bob Froehlick's note also tells volumes about the secret of his leadership success. The relationships he builds with his associates are not only professional, but often very personal. In a letter acknowledging Bob's book he says, "You may recall that Nancy and I have a summer home on Flathead Lake, which includes a guest house; so consider this an open invitation to come out and spend a few days with us when you feel it appropriate. The ideal time in Montana is during the months of July and August. This is a sincere invitation so please don't hesitate to give it a strong consideration."

This is vintage Ian Davidson—always cultivating new friendships, and always plugging Montana. Ask Tom Doherty, a Merrill Lynch executive from Boston, who first became acquainted with Ian when they served together on the Pacific Exchange board. They made the trip to Flathead Lake, succumbed to its charm, and are now summer neighbors of Ian and Nancy on Skidoo Lane. Or take Ray Wooldridge. Ray, then Chairman and CEO of Southwest Securities in Dallas, was on the NASD Board of Governors with Ian. When Ian wanted an outside director to join the DADCO Board of Directors to provide diversity of experience, Ray was selected. He and his wife, Ann, also spent vacation time with the Davidsons at Skidoo Lane. Now they, too, are summer Flathead residents, and their son, Peter, is with DAD's Public Finance area in Great Falls.

Incidently, the Dohertys and the Wooldridges, who were not acquainted before their common Flathead experience, spent the early part of the new millennium together vacationing abroad. Ian believes that friendships are meant to be shared.

May the story of the Dohertys and the Wooldridges also serve as a warning to Bob Froehlick should he accept the Davidson invitation. If you go to Flathead Lake, you also may find, as they did, that your lifestyle may experience a mid-life correction—but one you and your family will likely never regret.

As DADCO has grown, its structure has become increasingly complex. At the same time, though, it has rarely been spoken aloud, all have been conscious that the firm's management was also getting older. Occasional retirements of key people served as an unspoken reminder that time does not pause in its inexorable flight. The most recent Strategic Plan in 1997 was the first to address the problem of management succession, which the 1994 plane crash so clearly pinpointed. Thus, DADCO is not completely unprepared to face the day when Ian Davidson and other key players will, for whatever reason, step aside. At that time, others will be compelled to carry on.

As a new century and a new millennium dawns and the 20th century fades into history, we now turn to our crystal ball to anticipate some of the things that may lie ahead for the premier financial services organization in the Pacific Northwest.

Davidson home on Flathead Lake.

Whither Now?

At the outset, we planned to close our part of the DADCO story to coincide with the close of the 20th Century. But the man-made divisions of time into convenient segments we call months and years and centuries do not alter its inexorable march, and events continue to transpire, uninterrupted by its ebb and flow. The story of DADCO and its culture is a story without an end—at least in the foreseeable future.

Thus far, our story has covered only those events and happenings which have actually occurred. But the building of DADCO is not a done deal. It is still a work under construction. What we have been describing is a dynamic, growing organization which, only now, is starting to realize its ultimate potential. In the near-term, much backing and filling remains before it can truly become the dominant force in the securities industry by which all others in its region are measured.

There is ample retail development remaining in Washington, Oregon, and Utah to occupy the attention of those involved in the expansion of retail branches for the next several years. Nor have Idaho and Wyoming yet been saturated to the same extent as has Montana. For well into the next century, it seems reasonably safe to predict that D.A. Davidson & Co. will continue to grow in the retail area at a rate at least comparable to its historic growth. If past experience is a guide to the future, retail growth will stimulate growth in money management, trust services, investment banking, and specialist operations. If DADCO grows during the next five years at a rate comparable to that of the past five years, in 2004 it will manage almost $30 billion of customer assets; will have in excess of 50 offices employing nearly 1,000 people; will generate $250 million in revenues; and have capital of well over $100 million. As Andrew Davidson would say, these are "pretty awesome" projections by any measure.

In fact, based on what we have seen in the recent past—and what has already taken place in the early months of the year 2000—we feel comfortable predicting that these projections are likely to be exceeded by a considerable margin.

Skeptics might point out that the last five years have been a part of the longest bull stock market on record, when the price of common stocks reached unprecedented highs, and are not necessarily a reliable guide to their future performance. To such, we counter that the rate of growth at DADCO in the past five years has been consistent with that which the firm has experienced over the past 40 years, in the "down" years as well as the "up"; and that November 1987, the month following the biggest crash in the stock market since the Great Depression of 1929, still ranks as one of DAD's banner months in its 64-year history.

DAD has established itself as a solid performer that can withstand market volatility and is able to grow value for its customers in good times and bad.

Then there is the question of what comprises the region that DAD aspires to dominate. Thus far, only the six states of Montana, Wyoming, Idaho, Utah, Washington, and Oregon have been considered to comprise DAD's Northern Rockies/Pacific Northwest region. But how about Colorado and Alaska? Clearly, Colorado is a part of the Rocky Mountain region, and Alaska cannot be considered a part of any region but the Pacific Northwest. To a discerning observer, the topography of Colorado and the geographic location of its centers of population would seem to have far more in common in culture, transportation, and financial services with its neighbors to the north and west than those to the east and south. As to Alaska, the West Coast—Seattle in particular—is its only logical trade area.

If our assessment is correct, we would expect that it is only a question of time until these two states join the present six to complete the region in which DADCO aspires to be the premier firm. Once fully developed, there appears to be no plans, announced or contemplated, to move beyond them.

As it faces some formidable challenges in the future, DADCO enjoys one immense advantage: it is a privately-held corporation. All its stock is owned by its employees, either directly or through an employee stock ownership trust. The market for its stock is severely—and deliberately—limited. Active employment is a requirement for stock ownership. Once that relationship ceases, the firm has the opportunity to repurchase the stock, and the ex-employee is required to sell. Thus, DADCO is well-insulated against any attempt by outsiders to gain control, either by a friendly offer or a hostile takeover attempt. Present management has committed itself to maintain DADCO as a privately-held financial services business whose area of operation is restricted, except for its California specialist posts, to the Northern Rockies/Pacific Northwest geographic region. It aspires to be the best there is in the region in what it does.

That, in and of itself, does not eliminate the challenges it faces. It only makes it easier for DADCO to control its own destiny. While we are comfortable with those predictions of what may take place in the next few years, those involving a longer time frame are much harder to make with equal conviction. Many are likely to be shaped by discoveries and innovations, many yet unknown, which are beyond anyone's present capability to anticipate. For starters, there's the matter of new, and presently unknown, technology. Anyone daring today to make long-term predictions about the shape of the physical world of tomorrow is probably out of touch with reality. Who could have imagined at the start of the 20th Century that, by its end, man would have walked on the moon?...Have construction underway on a permanent work station in space, with instant voice and visual communication with the live humans who occupy it?...Would have perfected the technique for transplanting almost every major human organ but the brain from animals to humans, or from one human to another?

When this century began, there was no airplane, no radio, no television, few paved roads, and no movie theatres. Candles and kerosene lamps were the only source of light for most Americans. Only a handful of far-out dreamers could even imagine sending voice and visual messages by electricified wire or wave. Even now, there's a whole generation or two of oldies like me who are still scared to death of fax machines, e-mail, CAT scans and MRIs, and are totally ignorant of what is meant by bytes, CD-ROM, downloading, the Internet, and Web sites—or how they work. We are foreigners in a strange land at a computer convention. When a company like 3M (Minnesota Mining & Manufacturing) expects half of its growth five years from now to be from products that do not exist today, who among us is either brave or foolish enough to predict with conviction what DADCO may look like as a company ten years from now—let alone in AD 2100?

One concern which has already reared its head, however, is how DAD will handle the competitive trading cost advantage of buying and selling stocks and bonds through the Internet. It is a recent phenomenon which has its roots in the rise of the discount broker and the "unbundling" of transaction execution costs from the cost of research and all the other charges included in the traditional transaction fee which is added to the quoted price when buying a security. The Internet provides the means for amateur stock traders to retrieve information about, and buy or sell any stock or bond of their choosing, using tools equal to those available to the most experienced Wall Street professional.

There is little question that marketing via the Internet is likely to be the next great wave by which goods and services are moved from the producer to the consumer. Among the millions of total transactions made via the Internet in 1998 were more than 330,000 stock and bond trades every business day, according to an estimate in a leading business news magazine. While this is still only a tiny fraction of the business done by the entire industry, it is still sufficient to set off alarm signals at such venerable institutions as Merrill Lynch; particularly when the same source estimates that Charles Schwab, the largest discount broker, passed Merrill in 1998 in the number of investment transactions it handled during the year.

Internet trading is not likely to have any significant effect on the way a firm like D.A. Davidson & Co. does business in the near future. But it is virtually certain to do so as time goes by.

The Internet can seek out the lowest trading cost available and can arrange the trade. It cannot tell an investor what to buy—or why. Only someone who is thoroughly familiar with the individual's personal situation, financial goals, and tolerance for risk as well as the details of both the company which issues the proposed security and the economic climate prevailing at the time, can make a fully-informed decision as to whether a particular stock or bond is appropriate for a given customer at a given time. This is a time-honored rule which has been true for so long as the securities business has existed. For all, except those with a casino mentality, there has been nothing yet to indicate that this will change in the future.

As long as people retain their right to choose for themselves the products they feel will best provide the money to meet their future financial needs, they will need an accurate source of information in order to make an informed choice as to what is right for them. Unless they have the time and inclination to gather the information on their own from all the diverse sources from which it is available, and have the background of knowledge to digest its relevance to their individual situation, they will have to rely on others who do have such qualifications. That usually means a financial advisor who can devote his or her full time to such work. That is what a Davidson financial consultant does. As time passes, and the volume of knowledge continues to expand, the financial consultant's role is likely to continue to shift away from that of a product salesman to one of a true financial counselor and confidant. This may well alter the way a financial consultant is paid. Instead of receiving a commission based on the size and nature of the transaction, the consultant's pay is more likely to be based on the time devoted to research on a given case, and the value of the results which he or she helps the customer to realize.

As technology advances and its use becomes more widespread, the sheer volume of information available to all can surely be expected to grow. It is already beyond the capacity of most people to properly digest the volume of information now available to them to a point where they can grasp its significance to their situation. It can only be expected to get worse. We sometimes joke that many computer programs are out-of-date even before the public has a chance to buy them. Tragically, it is often a fact—and that becomes no joke! It emphasizes again the value of strong educational programs at all levels—not only as they relate to the formal public and private education of the general public, but also to the need for continuous education by all business in the specific requirements for the job for which an employee is hired, undergirded by on-going training to help them keep abreast of changes as they occur.

Therefore, it seems reasonable to assume that DADCO's emphasis on continuing education, for both employees and customers, actual and potential, can only be expected to take on increasing importance. We would expect the Department of Professional Development, instituted early in 1998, to grow in size and responsibility. The same will be true of Management Information Systems, dedicated to the training of personnel in the use of the computer and all its related technology. It not only teaches employees how to use all the appropriate marvels of technology—computer, fax machines, e-mail, etc.—to do their job better and faster, but it also provides expert assistance when any of them run into a glitch. All are designed to help those who assist customers to make better investment decisions which, in turn, grows financial value for everyone concerned in the process.

As we contemplate the future of DADCO, and consider those things likely to influence the direction it will take in the coming years, the ephemeral DADCO Culture pops up at virtually every turn. It is not an asset which shows on any balance sheet; yet Ian Davidson has repeatedly declared that he considers it worth more to the company's long-term prosperity than all the tangible assets shown on its balance sheet. It is that intangible quality that defines the character of a business, and represents the most reliable indicator as to what direction it can be expected to take in the future. The culture of DADCO is best defined in the character of Ian Davidson, himself: a warm and sincere concern for the welfare of those who do business with his firm, which transcends the importance of any personal profit he may derive for himself; respect for every associate who plays a part in DADCO's success, and his personal gratitude for their contribution; and a sincere desire to improve the quality of life for the citizens of every community in which the firm maintains a presence.

It starts with the quality of the people it hires. Each is carefully selected and trained for the job. They are well paid by the standards of the industry, with excellent benefits, and long-term security for those willing to consider their employment not just a job, but a long-term commitment. Every permanent employee has the chance to become an owner through an employee stock ownership trust, and each shares in DADCO profits each year. DADCO employees are not only co-workers, but are encouraged to become friends through frequent luncheons, receptions, and a variety of semi-social events throughout the year. They honor each other by recognizing their fellow workers for outstanding performance by nominating them for one of the company's Super Service Awards. These carry with them small cash rewards for a job well done.

Ian Davidson honors every employee in the Great Falls corporate headquarters with a bouquet of flowers on his or her birthday— delivered personally or through a major associate as his representative. Each is also his guest each year at a luncheon during the month of his or her anniversary with the firm. All employees who have joined DADCO since the preceding luncheon are also included as guests at these monthly luncheons. Similar events are encouraged in each detached branch office.

All these things are done routinely in an effort to help each employee to understand how his or her work relates to that of others in the firm, to help each to appreciate the importance of the work they do and how it relates to the level of success which the firm achieves, and to strengthen a sense of trust and respect between all at whatever level of responsibility they may occupy.

In short, the DADCO Culture can be defined as an environment in which all employees work together in an atmosphere of mutual trust and cooperation to help DADCO customers increase the value of the financial resources entrusted to its care; and, in the doing, enhance the quality of life for everyone in the community in which they live. Which brings us to a major challenge in the years ahead: *How does a firm maintain such a culture in the face of explosive growth?* In its formative days, what became the DADCO Culture—though not formally defined as such until much later—had its roots in the personality of Ian Davidson and his interest in people inherited from his mother. The people he selected to assist him reflected his values and shared his goals and dreams. They became partners with him to achieve common purposes which all had a part in shaping. It was a cooperative effort in which each became committed as an associate rather than only as a part of a group of conglomerate employees working in what is often almost a master-servant relationship.

Such a culture is not hard to maintain when a firm has only a few local offices located in an area where people share similar economic conditions with those who are products of the same social environment. But as it moved out of the confines of its familiar Montana heritage and into areas with different backgrounds and cultural mores, the job of maintaining close personal relationships with customers, employees and the communities of which they are a part, became more and more of a challenge. If for no other reason, the sheer growth in the number of people increasingly involved is enough to dilute the intimacy and personal trust between customer and DADCO, and between management and employees, which lie at the heart of the DADCO Culture. A meeting site to accommodate a few score people is much easier to find than one for several hundred. All can take part in the give-and-take of ideas between a few dozen participants; between hundreds, it becomes impossible. Already the company is finding that much of the personal camaraderie and mutual respect generated by discussions in a small group setting is severely diluted as the numbers grow. How to maintain this unique personal relationship in an ever-increasing work force made up of diverse individuals from a variety of social and economic environments is one of the most important future decisions DADCO will have to make.

It has already made a start toward addressing the problem. The first of three regional meetings—billed as the "Prairie Get-Together"—was held at Chico Hot Springs south of Livingston, Montana, near Yellowstone Park in early January 1999. Two other such gatherings, a spring meeting known as the "Mountain Wahootie" at Grouse Mountain Lodge at Whitefish, Montana; and a summer "Ocean Clambake" at a resort near Aberdeen, Washington, completed the series in 1999. All followed a common agenda. It was an experimental effort to find a format which will be a satisfactory substitute for the highly successful Spring Family Weekend which has played such a significant role in the past in nurturing the DADCO culture.

All the foreseeable challenges facing DADCO as it moves toward the 21st century—defining the limits of its region—coping with marketing and other innovations brought about by Internet trading, discount brokerage, etc.—preserving the DADCO Culture in an environment of explosive growth—pale beside the unspoken question which arises with increasing frequency in the mind of virtually everyone who has hitched his or her future to the fortunes of DADCO: *What happens when it faces a future without Ian Davidson?*

DADCO is rich in managerial talent. There are many with exceptional technical knowledge. There are some with fine managerial skills; and some who are excellent motivators of people. But Ian Davidson has proven himself to be a master of all. Rare, indeed, are those individuals who can dream a dream, yet master the details of making it become a reality; who can assemble a team to do a job, exert the discipline necessary to get it done, and still retain their fierce loyalty. Not only has Ian done it, but he has done it so humbly that those involved truly feel that they are working *with* him to accomplish *their* goal instead of working *for* him to attain *his* goal.

The great unknown facing DADCO is what happens when Ian Davidson steps aside? So long as he is physically able, he will almost certainly exert a major influence on the future direction of the firm. It has been too great a part of his life for far too long. But there will come a time down the road when DADCO will be faced with a future without his guiding hand. What then?

It would be naive to close one's eyes to the profound effect it will have when it does take place. The realization of that fact has already caused some uneasiness. It is inevitable that there will be some jockeying for position when it does occur. It is likely to grow as time passes.

The only member of Ian's direct family who is presently associated actively with DADCO is his son, Andrew, a portfolio manager at Financial Aims. Since his graduation from the University of Montana, Andrew has been carefully groomed for a career in the securities business. He has been through the training school for new financial consultants. He has had experience with two firms other than DAD; first as a retail broker, then as a portfolio money manager. Since 1993, he has been a money manager at Financial Aims. He has also worked closely with his father in the management of the accounts of many of Ian's personal clients. He has already been able to establish a reputation for astuteness and creativity with many of them. Increasingly, he has served as a contributing member of numerous company committees, including Research and Investment.

Ian has long been an outspoken proponent of nepotism. Throughout DAD there are many successful parent-sibling combinations. However, this by no means makes Andrew Davidson the favored choice to succeed his father at his retirement. As with any father, it is logical to assume that this might be a long-held desire of Ian Davidson. But the continued success of the firm he has built will weigh far more heavily in the final selection than sibling love and loyalty. Unless Ian, and those who will join with him to make the final choice, are convinced that Andrew is the best choice to continue the work his father has so successfully commenced, it is highly unlikely that he will be chosen. Much will depend on the time and conditions which exist at the time the choice is made.

The only certain prediction at this time seems to be that Andrew will occupy a position of importance in the future plans of DADCO.

In the near-term, it appears to be quite certain that no major change in present direction is imminent. Ian Davidson is firmly in charge; and will likely continue to be so as long as his health permits and he desires to remain active. It is hard to imagine that he will precipitately ride off into the sunset, even after he steps aside and relinquishes the reins of day-to-day decision-making to a younger successor. He has, however, reached the time-honored age for retirement; and both he and Nancy are increasingly wooed by the freedom from everyday pressures of the job offered by their retreat on Flathead Lake, and the opportunity to visit more frequently with the interesting friends they have made in all parts of the country. They have tried to solve the latter problem by introducing some of them to the Flathead magic and helping them to find suitable vacation property sites nearby.

Ian Davidson has put together an outstanding team of associates who share his goals, his value system, and service ideals. Each has been well tested and has proved his or her ability by their performance. Despite internal changes which may occur in the responsibilities of its leaders, the future of DADCO as the regional leader in the securities industry seems bright and secure.

Epilogue

In the last chapter we speculated on some foreseeable problems facing DADCO in the new century. At the time, we were unaware that forces were already at work which would bring the problem of choosing a new Chief Executive Officer to succeed Ian Davidson to the front burner and place it at the top of its agenda.

Early in February, 1999, in a system-wide conference call, Ian announced his intention to relinquish his responsibilities as CEO of DADCO. The announcement was timed to coincide with the meeting of the Chairman's Council the following week. It was designed to give him an opportunity to discuss, and fully explain in person all the reasons for the decision at that time to the largest gathering of the top company leaders which occur during the year.

The decision to ease off was not made in haste or on the spur of the moment. It had been the subject of much thought for some time. After all, he had held the job for 41 years, almost—if not in fact—a record in the securities industry. He had observed his 67th birthday in early December. Nancy, his family, and several of his close personal friends had been gently suggesting for some time that he consider easing off. He has enjoyed excellent health over the years, but recently there has been evidence that his 12-hour, 300-plus days-a-year schedule is starting to take its toll. They wanted him to have a chance to pursue other personal interests while he could still enjoy them. Daily 7:00 AM meetings, 3:00 PM lunches on the fly; interminable telephone conversations, interspersed with pressure-packed meetings; a steady stream of daily personal interviews and conferences; 7:00 PM dinners interrupted by more phone calls—this has been the pattern of Ian Davidson's daily work schedule for the better part of half a century. In the meantime, Lauren and Tim are living in the San Francisco Bay Area where Nicholas and Ian need a lot of frequent grand-parenting. The same is true of Sydney and Paul, recent immigrants to the Minneapolis area from Great Falls when Paul was a casualty of the sale of Buttrey Foods to Albertson's. This left a huge void in the lives of Ian and Nancy who are devoted to Ryan, Casey, Alex and

The Davidson family in 1985. Left to right: Ian, Sydney, Lauren, Andrew and Nancy.

Lucas. The arrival of Zachary in April only compounds their need for more leisure time for travel; and, of course, there is also Abigail, and now little Andrew, in Great Falls who deserve equal time. Over the years, Nancy and Ian have piled up a lot of frequent-flyer miles from trips they have made on behalf of industry or philanthropic organizations to which they have devoted a great deal of time. Ian's ease-off will allow them the opportunity to use those free flying miles to spend time with both sets of grandsons, when they are not grandparenting some or all the grandchildren at Flathead Lake.

Ian, of course, recognizes that, as it happens at some point to everyone, he cannot go on forever. There will come a time when DADCO will have to face a future without his guiding hand at its helm. Far better that the inevitable changes—and their attendant turmoil—occur on his schedule and on his terms than to face a crisis situation where decisions might have to be made in haste. By starting the process in an atmosphere of calm deliberation, his replacement can be chosen under his guidance by consensus among those most affected. The new CEO will then have the chance to demonstrate his management style. He will be able to settle in with a new team and provide assurance to all that the DADCO Culture is secure in their hands. Ian is adamant that the most important ingredient in that culture is the independent status of DADCO. He has no interest in selling out to some New York wirehouse, banking conglomerate, or other national financial behemoth. As Ian told a Billings newspaper reporter in a feature story about DADCO in July 1998, "So you get two or three times book (when you sell). Five years from now, you'll have two or three times book anyway...We get a bunch of money on our stock, and then what do we do? Get a phone call from New York and hear, 'By the way, we just sublet your building in Great Falls, so why don't you clean out your office?' There's more to the world than hard dollars in market values that fluctuate. What would happen to our 600 people?"

Ian recognizes that the time has come to start the inevitable transition of power. But he has devoted more than 40 years of his life to building an organization which has grown to a position of pre-eminence and influence in its industry. He has been joined in the effort by hundreds of loyal associates, many of whom have devoted much of their working life to it. He is deeply indebted to them for their loyalty and devotion. He will welcome the relief from the responsibilities of day-to-day management, and the opportunity it affords to spend time with grandchildren at the lake, or traveling to exotic, far-away places with exhilarating friends from all parts of the country.

But all of this would turn to dross should a drastic change in management style of philosophy result in the destruction of all he has worked to achieve. The unique DADCO Culture lies at the heart of its success. The foundation for the transition was laid out in the 1996 strategic Plan. Shortly following Ian's announcement, a Search Committee started the selection process by choosing Heidricks & Struggles, a nationally recognized executive search firm, to assist it. Candidates from both within and without the company were considered in an attempt to find the best person available to continue the development of DADCO. The new CEO, and an enlarged Board of Directors and Management Committee, will define new duties, responsibilities, and lines of accountability for each one in a decision-making role.

After many hours reviewing the qualifications of dozens of potential candidates brought to it by Heidricks & Struggles, the Search Committee again found its person within the firm's own ranks. Again, it was Vinney Purpura, the President of D.A. Davidson & Co. His unanimous choice was announced before a group of more than 100 DADCO shareholders and co-workers to a standing ovation on January 21. It was a very popular choice among both the rank and file of DADCO employees, and its customers.

This is not to say that there may not be some second thoughts, particularly among those who have joined DADCO in recent years. Many of them came from situations where changes had occurred which seemed to signal a shift in the basic values of the firm they were with. Some will wonder if: "here we go again!" The same is true of some of their customers. It is only natural that this would be so.

The uneasiness of those who have grown over the years with DAD is directed more to a concern as to how well the one chosen to succeed Ian is able to fill the big shoes he will leave. He has left some large footprints on the entire industry. It will take some doing to follow in them.

Ian Davidson is a humble man who is quick to shift the credit for the DADCO success from himself to his associates. With all his modesty, however, Ian Davidson cannot gainsay the fact that he does have an unusual and uncommon talent for leadership. As he has often observed, leadership is not a status conferred by one person on another. Rather, it is a quality which one possesses that enables one to make right decisions and to inspire others to follow his lead to reach the goals he sets. True leadership is more an art than a science. A person can go to school to learn the principles of good management. He can understudy at the feet of good managers and see how they do it. But, in the end, it is those intangible qualities of sensitivity to the needs of all the constituencies they serve, confidence they inspire in their ability to make right decisions and to do the right thing, and the commitment they demonstrate to the values which defines their culture that stamps them as a true leader.

Vinney Purpura is a clone of Ian Davidson so far as his commitment to the DADCO Culture is concerned. It is safe to assume that the team he picks will share the same commitment. Therefore, it would seem the future of the DADCO Culture seems to be secure when Ian Davidson steps down and a new team takes over. The transition is likely to be smooth and gradual, and those who have done business with DAD over the years will probably see little that is changed as it moves into a new century of growth and service.

It will be the same old Sally in a brand spankin' new and modern outfit. It is a fitting culmination of Ian Davidson's long-held hope and dream.

If, in our story, I seem to have painted Ian Davidson as some kind of Superman, it is only because he fits the bill. Without apology, I would record that so far as I am concerned, he is a *super* human being and a *super* leader! Like all of us, he has his human faults and idiosyncrasies.

He sometimes drives Nancy to distraction with his fascination for memorabilia. He is a collector—a human packrat of sorts. He saves things just because they once served him well and they bring back pleasant memories. By contrast, to Nancy today's newspaper is ancient news by noon and a candidate for the trash bin. If something is not used or worn on a regular basis, it is likely to wind up at Goodwill. To her, old things take up useful space that can be better used for things of more immediate use. Unless they are antique collectibles, they are junk—and she abhors junk! Ian is forever retrieving some cherished treasure from the waste container after Nancy has been on a cleaning spree. It is a sort of family cat-and-mouse routine that has added spice to their happy marriage.

In his business, Ian is a stickler for accuracy, honest appraisal and full and complete disclosure. He will not tolerate the slightest mistreatment of a customer, either through inadvertent thoughtlessness or by deliberate action or misrepresentation. He will not allow any customer to suffer any loss, for any reason, if it is caused by anything anyone in the company did or failed to do. Yet he does any necessary disciplining in private, always conscious of the feelings of the one being disciplined. If any employee is accused of any wrongdoing that cannot be substantiated by fact, Ian will be equally vigorous in defending them.

Ian makes it a priority to meet and get to know every new employee, no matter where located, as early as possible in their career at DADCO. Many of them meet him during the employment screening process. All get personally-signed cards on birthdays, at Christmas, and other significant occasions. He hosts a luncheon each month at the Great Falls headquarters for any in the then-current Executive Training Class, as well as all those who joined the firm in any department within the past month. The only purpose is to provide a vehicle for those invited to become acquainted with, and learn something about, others with whom they work.

He glories in the company-wide meetings held each year which attempt to bring together everyone in the entire firm. Spouses are always included at every DADCO function. One each year is geared to the entire family, with a special program arranged specifically for the children. These meetings have played a major part in establishing and defining the DADCO culture which places families and communities and people at the center of its reason for existence. The day DADCO gets so big that it can no longer maintain the camaraderie and dedication generated by these meetings will likely be the day Ian Davidson will conclude that his "good little Montana firm" has gotten too big. It is something future management should carefully consider in its long range planning.

It was during a break between sessions at one of its Annual Meetings some years ago that Johan Miller made a casual remark that seems to summarize the DADCO story in a nutshell. We were standing together watching some 300 of the most successful financial consultants in the Pacific Northwest—many of whom are among the leading citizens in their respective communities—mill around discussing the presentation they had just heard from one of America's foremost economic analysts. Suddenly, he turned and, almost in awe at what he saw unfolding before him, said, "If Dave Davidson could walk into this room right now, and see what that little office he started so many years ago has become, he'd never, in his wildest imagination, believe it."

DADCO's shadow looms ever larger in the financial services industry in the Northern Rockies/Pacific Northwest and lengthens with each passing day. But as shadows grow longer and the sun passes its zenith, so the shadow cast by Ian Davidson on an ever larger area grows longer and longer as he marches toward the twilight years of a great career. And up there somewhere in the Great Beyond, if David Adams Davidson were able to pause briefly from his self-imposed job of posting current stock prices on heavenly companies on that great Quote Board in the Sky, to gaze down on the 21st Century DADCO that Gibson Associates has become, he'd certainly echo Johan's sentiments in spades.

Mother Scottie, however, would simply smile a knowing smile of deep satisfaction as she and Uncle Chuck continue to orient new arrivals at the Pearly Gates and explain the rules of celestial citizenship to them.

She would be pleased, but not surprised. She knew all along that her boy, Ian, was someone special … and destined to leave his mark on all he touched.

History Appendix

Here my tale of DADCO ends, but the *story* continues.

Ian Davidson has relinquished the reins as the Chief Executive Officer of the Davidson Companies to Vinney Purpura and has moved upstairs to the Chairman's suite, where he will serve as a spokesman for the Company in industry affairs and as its senior statesman in the region it serves.

Bill Johnstone has joined Vinney in the corporate suite as the President of D.A. Davidson & Co., the original Davidson Company, and the largest of its four units. Bill's impressive credentials as a former CEO of Rauscher Pierce & Refnes, one of the nation's leading regional securities firms, and as the Managing Partner of Dorsey & Whitney, one of the nation's largest legal establishments, does much to confirm the firm's position as one of America's premier financial services organizations.

Even before the changes in leadership, the name had undergone change. From its humble beginnings as E.J. Gibson & Co., and progressing through Gibson Associates, D.A. Davidson & Co., and finally DADCO, the *Davidson* name continues to gain increasing recognition beyond its original Montana borders. To capitalize on its reputation as a name synonomous with excellence in its field; and to simplify the recognition of each unit as a part of the whole, Financial Aims Corporation has become Davidson Investment Advisors, and DADCO TRAVEL has become Davidson Travel. TrustCorp underwent a similar change in 1997 when it became Davidson Trust Co. Together with D.A. Davidson & Co., they comprise the DAVIDSON COMPANIES, formerly known as DADCO, Inc.

The net effect of these changes has been largely cosmetic. It has in no way slowed the firm's spectacular growth. The final figures in the company's 2000 Annual Report showed new records set in almost every category by which the progress of financial services companies are measured. Vinney Purpura, Bill Johnstone, and their entire crew are well-positioned to continue the pattern of growth so brilliantly established by Ian Davidson and his associates in the economic and social turmoil of the 1960s, and carefully nurtured in all the years since.

What follows is a synopsis of the significant milestones in the company's history.

SIGNIFICANT MILESTONES ... 1935 through 2000

1935-58: *The Gibson Years*

5/3/1935   Brokerage firm E.J. Gibson, Inc. opens for business in Butte, Montana.

9/30/1935   Dow Jones Industrial Average (DJIA) is at 131.92.

10/10/1935   D.A. (David Adams) Davidson of Great Falls, Montana, is elected Director of E.J. Gibson, Inc.

1935

D.A. Davidson opens first and only E.J. Gibson branch office in Great Falls, Montana.

10/14/1935   D.A. Davidson opens first and only E.J. Gibson branch office in Great Falls' one-story Steele Building (present lobby of Davidson Building).

1/3/1936   D.A. Davidson elected Second Vice President in charge of E.J. Gibson Great Falls branch.

2/13/1937   E.J. Gibson changes corporate name to Gibson Associates and becomes member of the Chicago Board of Trade.

9/18/1938   Gibson stockholders' meeting held in Great Falls for first time.

1941

D.A. Davidson and family buy all stock of Gibson Associates from shareholders in Butte and Spokane, and move headquarters to Great Falls.

May/June 1941   D.A. Davidson and family buy all stock of Gibson Associates from shareholders in Butte and Spokane, move headquarters to Great Falls, and sell Butte office to J.A. Hogle of Salt Lake City, Charles and Harry Davidson, brothers of D.A. Davidson, are elected Directors.

9/29/1945   DJIA reaches 181.71.

9/30/1955   A decade later, DJIA is 466.62.

2/1958   Ian B. Davidson joins his father D.A. Davidson and Secretary/Cashier Ann Weldele as third full-time Gibson employee. Firm's net worth is $33,000. Annual gross income (1957) is $17,000.

6/10/1958   Ian B. Davidson elected Gibson Director and Secretary-Treasurer. David S. Davidson elected Director.

9/1/1958	Gibson Associates joins the Pacific Coast Stock Exchange (Los Angeles Division) as a corporate member, gaining access to other major stock exchanges.
2/4/1959	Gibson Associates renamed D.A. Davidson & Co. (DAD), honoring David Adams Davidson and reflecting the firm's heritage.
5/4/1959	First DAD branch office — staffed by a secretary and a single broker/manager (James E. Howeth) — opens on the second floor of Helena's Power Block.

1959

Gibson Associates is renamed D.A. Davidson & Co. (DAD).

3/1960	Headquarters and branch employee count reaches eight, including new Great Falls hire William S. Macfadden, Jr., an experienced broker.
6/1960	DAD main office moves from Steele Building across the street to ground floor location in the Great Falls National Bank Building (now Norwest Bank).
4/1961	Johan Miller replaces retiring Secretary/Treasurer Ann Weldele (a 23-year employee). Miller receives on-the-job training as DAD's first Account Executive Trainee.
2/1964	Robert A. Braig joins DAD in Missoula.
5/1965	Third DAD office, managed by Warren E. Drew, opens in Florence Hotel in Missoula. Total DAD employment reaches thirty-one; company net worth reaches $165,000.
9/30/1965	DJIA reaches 930.58.
10/1965	Ian B. Davidson buys Steele Building in Great Falls (original company location) in anticipation of company move.
7/1966	DAD moves into new quarters in Steele Building (street-level space now occupied by the DAD's Great Falls sales office).
1/1968	Montana's first full-service Municipal Bond Department opens at DAD, under direction of new hire and DAD Vice President Eugene S. Hufford. Hufford brings eleven years of municipal bond experience to the firm. Total employees in three offices reaches forty; net worth reaches $450,000.

4/22/1968	Butte branch opens in its present location, becoming DAD's fourth office. Charles W. Bowers named manager.
6/1968	Ian B. Davidson named DAD President.

1969-85: *Branching Out*

4/1969	CPA Stu Nicholson joins DAD; becomes Vice President of Operations in 1970.
11/1969	With four-story addition, the Steele Building — renamed the Davidson Building — becomes a major downtown structure in Great Falls.
6/1970	DAD joins Midwest Stock Exchange, expanding its regional transaction coverage. D.A. Davidson elected DAD Chairman; Ian B. Davidson, President; and William S. Macfadden, Executive Vice President.
10/16/1970	Having just celebrated the thirty-fifth anniversary of the firm bearing his name, D.A. Davidson dies at age 76.
12/1970	Ian B. Davidson named DAD Chairman, CEO, and President.
2/1971	DAD contracts with the Midwest Stock Exchange Service Bureau to update the firm's brokerage accounting system. Net worth passes $850,000, with fifty-seven employees.
11/1972	Fifth DAD branch office opens in Securities Building in Billings, Montana. Manager is Charles W. Bowers. DAD employment reaches seventy-two, including twenty-seven Investment Executives.
5/15/1974	DAD sells Chicago Board of Trade membership, terminating company involvement in the commodities business.

1968

Montana's first full-service Municipal Bond Department opens at DAD. Ian B. Davidson is named DAD President. Total DAD employees number forty.

1970

DAD joins the Midwest Stock Exchange. D.A. Davidson dies at age 76.

8/1974	With purchase of Kalispell office of San Francisco investment firm Birr, Wilson, DAD moves into northwestern Montana with sixth branch. Robert A. Braig named branch manager. DAD net worth reaches $1 million.
1/1975	DAD buys Financial Aims Corporation, a Minneapolis-based financial planning firm and registered investment advisor, from Bill Preston. Company moves to Great Falls as a wholly owned DAD subsidiary, with Bill Preston remaining as President.
9/29/1975	DJIA is at 793.88 down 137 from a decade ago.

1975

DAD buys Financial Aims Corporation, moving the company from Minneapolis to Great Falls.

7/1977	DAD's seventh branch opens in Bozeman, Montana, on Main Street. Manager is David E. Wagner. DAD employment reaches ninety-five; net worth reaches $1.8 million.
7/1978	Eighth DAD branch office opens in Havre, Montana, a purchase form the St. Louis investment firm of Edward D. Jones & Co. Clark Henderson named manager.
9/1980	DAD opens first branch outside Montana-in Williston, North Dakota. Office opens in Rolfstad Building and moves to Old Post Office Building, with Robert Petersen as manager. DAD net worth reaches $4.6 million.
10/1980	*Forbes* Magazine profiles DAD; calls company the "quintessential regional brokerage firm."

1980

First DAD branch opens outside Montana. DAD net worth reaches $4.6 million.

1/1982	William S. Macfadden named President of Financial Aims Corporation. Assets under management by this growing DAD subsidiary pass $10 million.
8/1982	L. Bruce Madsen named DAD President. Ian B. Davidson remains Chairman and CEO.

4/1983	DAD is largest brokerage firm domiciled in the Pacific Northwest, based on capital resources. DAD total capital exceeds $8 million; 156 people are employed in nine offices.

1983

With total capital exceeding $8 million, DAD becomes the largest brokerage firm domiciled in the Pacific Northwest, based on capital resources.

4/1984	DAD expands service area to northern Idaho and eastern Washington with new branch in Moscow, Idaho, managed by John Dayries.
12/1984	Lewiston, Idaho office purchased from Shearson American Express, expanding DAD coverage into northern Idaho. A.C. "Bud" Nelson named acting manager.
8/1985	DAD CEO Ian. B. Davidson named Executive of the Year by Western Business for company and employee leadership and commitment to community, state, and region.
9/1985	DAD capital approaches $12 million. Company employs 185 people in three states, remaining the largest firm in the Pacific Northwest based on capital resources.

1985

In its fiftieth year, DAD employs 185 people in three states. DAD capital approaches $12 million.

9/29/1985	DJIA reaches 1328.63.
10/14/1985	DAD celebrates its fiftieth year with a company party in Great Falls.
10/21/1985	Due to reputation and financial strength, DAD selected (from among several firms) by the Board of Governors of the Pacific Stock Exchange in San Francisco to operate a Specialist Post. Paul Sweeney named DAD Specialist.

1986-94:   *Accolades*

1/6/1986	DAD's third Idaho office opens in Coeur d'Alene, with Bryan Ross as manager.

| 2/1986 | Changing Times, the Kiplinger magazine, names DAD one of the seven leading regional investment firms in the United States. |

1986

DAD is named one of seven leading regional investment firms in U.S. Newly formed DADCO purchases Trust Corporation of Montana.

| 3/31/1986 | DAD Specialist Post #81 on the Pacific Stock Exchange ranks highest among all West Cost Specialist Posts. |

| 5/8/1986 | New holding company — DADCO — formed as parent company of DAD and Financial Aims Corporation. |

| 6/16/1986 | DADCO buys Trust Corporation of Montana, an independent trust company, from bank of Montana System. Bob Bragg named President. |

| 7/18/1986 | Williston, North Dakota office closes. Jeff Nesset, manager, transfers to Lewiston, ID. |

| 9/1986 | DAD-funded investment classes begin at University of Montana, continue at Montana State University (implemented in 1985). |

| 10/1986 | DAD establishes first intern program; university students participate (for credit) in DAD broker training. |

| 11/15/1986 | Wholly financed by DAD, life-size statue of Charles M. Russell dedicated in downtown Great Falls. |

| 3/1987 | DAD Corporate Finance Department established under management of Mark Semmens, former Bond Program Manager for the Montana Economic Development Board. |

1987

DAD funds and co-develops the public television program "Wall Street in the Rockies," carried on PBS throughout the northern Rockies. DAD posts record month in October, despite record stock market decline.

| 4/1987 | DAD Insurance Department created under management of John Bebee, former Chief Deputy Insurance Commissioner of Montana. |

| 5/1987 | Security Bank Building in Billings, Montana renamed the D.A. Davidson Building (current Billings DAD location). |

6/1987	In conjunction with Montana State University, DAD develops public television program "Wall Street in the Rockies." Funded by DAD, the program is carried on PBS throughout the northern Rockies.
8/1987	DAD's Kalispell branch celebrates its thirteenth year, expanding its offices on the first floor of the downtown KM Building.
9/1987	DAD obtains second Specialist Post on the Pacific Stock Exchange in San Francisco.
9/9/1987	Ian B. Davidson named to Board of Governors of Pacific Stock Exchange.
9/25/1987	The three DADCO companies post combined record revenues and record net income, employing 225 people in Montana, Idaho, and California. Total capital exceeds $16 million.
10/14/1987	Trust Corporation and Financial Aims Corporation host open houses at expanded headquarters in the Great Falls Davidson Building, third floor.
10/19/1987	Record stock market decline.
10/31/1987	DAD posts best month in its history, due to conservative investment philosophy.
12/1987	DAD's Lewiston, Idaho office moves to new location in historic train station. Throughout 1987, Moscow, Coeur d'Alene, Bozeman office expand and remodel.
1/15/1988	Of seventy-two Specialist Posts on floor of Pacific Stock Exchange, DAD specialist Post #81 ranks first for four quarters of 1987.
2/17/1988	Ian B. Davidson becomes first recipient of Neil S. Bucklew Presidential Service Award from University of Montana.
9/31/1988	DAD closes its Moscow office, consolidating northern Idaho activities in Coeur d'Alene and Lewiston. Capital approaches $18 million, marking thirty consecutive years of increased capital for DADCO companies.

> **1988**
>
> *DAD Specialist Post #81 ranks first of seventy-two Posts on Pacific Stock Exchange. Forbes recognizes DAD as a leading investment firm serving the individual investor.*

11/14/1988	Forbes recognizes DAD as a leading investment firm serving the individual investor.
12/1988	Ian B. Davidson elected to Board of Directors of Securities Industry Association, representing the Pacific Northwest.
2/17/1989	Pacific Stock Exchange selects DAD to operate a new Post in Los Angeles, the third DAD Specialist Post.
5/3/1989	DAD initiates "Take Stock in Montana" day, endorsed by the Governor of Montana. More than a thousand Montanans buy $14 million total in stock in Montana-based companies and national companies employing Montanans.
5/1989	State of Idaho grants first-ever out-of-state trust charter to Trust Corporation of Montana.
9/29/'998	Total capital exceeds $20 million.
10/1989	Eugene P. Lewis named President and CEO of Financial Aims Corporation, succeeding William S. Macfadden.
11/30/1989	L. Bruce Madsen retires as DAD President and COO after twenty-one years with company; he remains on the Board of Directors.
12/11/1989	Robert A. Braig, DAD Senior Vice President and Kalispell Branch Manager, elected Director of Retail Branches. Greg Barkus assumes Braig's branch manager duties. Twenty-one Investment Executives and key staff recognized for performance.

1989

The State of Idaho grants its first-ever out-of-state trust charter to Trust Corporation of Montana.

1990-93: *New Decade, New Growth*

2/1990	Trust Corporation of Montana changes name to TrustCorp, reflecting multistate service area.
2/1990	Guy C. Blackwell, former executive officer of AG Edwards and Sons, is named President and Chief Operating Officer of DAD. His tenure is brief; he resigns and returns to Nevada in June 1990.

1990

DAD acquires its fifth Specialist Post on the Pacific Stock Exchange. Capital passes $20.3 million; total client assets under management reach $561 million.

6/1990	DAD acquires fourth Specialist Post on Pacific Stock Exchange.
8/1990	DAD acquires fifth Specialist Post on Pacific Stock Exchange-Specialist Post #31 in Los Angeles.
9/6/1990	Vincent M. Purpura elected President and Chief Operating Officer of DAD, the fifth person in DAD history to serve as company President.
9/28/1990	Capital passes $20.3 million; total client assets under management reach $561 million.
11/1/1990	William S. Macfadden, Jr.-Chairman of the Board of Financial Aims Corporation and DADCO's fifth employee-retires after thirty years of service.
1/1/1991	DAD obtains excess customer insurance from Lloyd's of London, protecting all DAD accounts up to $4.5 million. Coverage includes SIPC coverage for $500,000 and customer coverage of $2 million.
1/1991	DAD installs ILX Information System for quick retrieval of market, investment, and portfolio information by Investment Executives.

Tim Owen named Vice President and Manager of DAD's Bozeman office. Vice President, Phil Smith, manager for nine years, remains on office staff.

Ian B. Davidson, DADCO Chairman and CEO, elected Vice Chairman-Elect of the Pacific Stock Exchange. He will become Vice Chairman in 1992.

2/4/1991	Robert M. Retz, former manager of Great Falls office of Dain Bosworth, Inc., joins DAD as Senior Vice President and Director of Retail Branch Offices.
2/15/1991	DAD acquires sixth Specialist Post (with David Hultman, Specialist) on Pacific Stock Exchange-four Posts in San Francisco and two in Los Angeles.

1991

DAD acquires its sixth Specialist Post on the Pacific Stock Exchange, for a total of four in San Francisco and two in Los Angeles. The three DADCO companies employ 240 people, including staff at thirteen DAD retail offices in three states.

3/28/1991	DADCO companies remain in exceptionally strong financial condition.
3/1991	Scott Wink named Vice President and Manager of DAD's Havre (Montana) office. Vice President Mic Armon, manager for ten years, transfers to Coeur d'Alene branch.
5/1991	Bill Beaman, Helena, and Reyne Grinsteinner, Trust Corp (Great Falls) return from active duty in the Persian Gulf.
8/23/1991	DAD expands into Wyoming—and adds nine employees —with offices in Cody, Gillette, and Jackson. All three offices acquired from Dean Witter Reynolds.
9/27/1991	Total capital approaches $21.6 million, with more than $2.4 billion in client assets under management. The three DADCO companies employ 240 people, including staff at thirteen DAD retail offices in three states.
10/1991	Dave Kuhns named Vice President and Manager of DAD's Billings office. Vice President Phil Boggio, manager for thirteen years, remains on office staff.
12/1991	Keith Radabah joins TrustCorp as Vice President and Trust Officer, responsible for trust accounts in Western Montana and the Flathead Valley.
1/1992	Ian B. Davidson elected Vice Chairman of Executive Committee of Pacific Stock Exchange.
2/1992	*USA Today* features DAD as model regional investment firm.
5/1992	Ian and Nancy Davidson donate $1 million to University of Montana Honors College.

Paul Eichwald named Manager of DAD's Missoula office, replacing ten-year manager Dick Hughes.

Bob Bragg, President of TrustCorp, becomes Montanan's first Certified Business Appraiser.

1992

DADCO acquires DADCO TRAVEL, a full-service travel agency in Great Falls. Ian and Nancy Davidson donate $1 million to the University of Montana Honors College.

6/5/1992	DAD's fourteenth branch office—and first office in Washington—opens in the historic Old City Hall in downtown Spokane. Bob Cummings named Vice President and Manager.
9/26/1992	DAD acquires DADCO TRAVEL, a full-service travel agency located in Great Falls' Davidson Building. Darrell Block named President of the company, DADCO's fourth subsidiary.
9/1992	DAD ranks 123rd largest of 5,386 U.S. securities firms, based on capital of $24.6 million. DADCO employees number 275.
10/1992	L. Bruce Madsen, former President and COO of DADCO and DAD, rejoins DADCO as Vice-Chairman.
11/1992	DAD introduces DADVANTAGE Asset Management Plan.
1/1993	Ian B. Davidson elected to NASD Board of Governors for three-year term, representing the Pacific Northwest.
3/1993	DAD establishes $50,000 annual student investment fund at University of Idaho College of Business and Economics. Fred Dickson joins DAD as Research Director.
4/1993	Dave Milbrath joins DAD in Spokane as Senior Vice President, Investments.
5/1993	*Newsweek* features Ian B. Davidson and DADCO in major news article. DADCO holds Strategic Planning Conference—the fifth companywide planning meeting since 1981—attended by fourteen representatives from the four DADCO companies.
8/1993	With addition of two Pacific Stock Exchange Posts in Los Angeles-for a total of four each in Los Angeles and San Francisco-DAD becomes largest Specialist operation on the Exchange.

> # 1993 ...
>
> *Ian B. Davidson elected to NASD Board of Governors for three-year term. With eight Specialist Posts, DAD becomes the largest Specialist operation on the Pacific Stock Exchange.*

9/1993	Raymond E. Wooldridge, President and CEO of Southwest Securities Group in Dallas, Texas, elected first outside director of DAD and DADCO Board of Directors.
	Capital reaches record $28.5 million. DADCO employees number 322. Financial Aims and TrustCorp post records.
	DAD establishes $50,000 annual student investment fund at Washington State University, Pullman, Washington.
11/1/1993	Full-service DAD branch office opens in Hamilton, Montana. Jim Moerkerke named Vice President, Branch Manager.
11/1993	Michael Morrison joins DADCO TRAVEL as Vice President. Agency moves into expanded quarters in Davidson Building and installs state-of-the-art computerized reservation system.

> **■ ■ ■ ■**
> *Full-service DAD branch office — the company's fifteenth — opens in Hamilton, Montana.*

12/1993	Big Sky Business Review, monthly publication of Great Falls Tribune, profiles DADCO and Ian B. Davidson.

1994-95: *Tragedy and Beyond*

3/1994	State of Washington grants trust powers to TrustCorp.
6/1994	Jan Nace, DAD Vice President, named Cody Branch Manager.
7/1994	Full-service DAD office opens in Wenatchee, Washington—the state's second DAD office—with Rob Johnson as Vice President and Manager.
8/1994	DAD establishes $50,000 annual student investment fund at Carroll College, Helena, Montana.
9/1994	DAD's Coeur d'Alene branch office moves to new quarters in the Spokesman Review Building.

> **1994...**
> *A Full-service DAD office opens in Wenatchee, Washington — the state's second DAD office. Capital reaches $31.5 million.*

For eleventh consecutive year, DAD sponsors annual women's Rankin Run in Great Falls. Proceeds go to YWCA.

Capital reaches $31.5 million. DADCO employees number 350 and serve more than a hundred thousand accounts.

11/4/1994	Seventeenth DAD office opens in Boise, Idaho—Idaho's third—staffed by four Investment Executives and a Registered Assistant. Tom Zemlicka named Vice President and Branch Manager.

11/8/1994   DADCO plane crashes shortly after takeoff from Great Falls International Airport, killing executives Eugene P. Lewis, President, Financial Aims Corporation; Robert B. Bragg, President, TrustCorp; and Donald C. Knutson, Senior Vice President, TrustCorp. Pilot Harry Graf also dies.

> ....
> *The DADCO plane crashes shortly after takeoff from Great Falls International Airport on November 8, killing DADCO executives Eugene P. Lewis, Robert B. Bragg, and Donald C. Knutson.*

11/11/1994   Family funeral services and DADCO memorial service held in Great Falls for DADCO executives and pilot killed in November 8 crash. More than 700 people attend memorial service for DADCO employees, family members, and friends.

11/18/1994   DAD's Gillette office moves to 100 E. Fourth Street.

12/1994   Michael Morrison named President of DADCO TRAVEL.

1/1995   With 1995 NASD election, Ian B. Davidson becomes first executive from Pacific Northwest to chair NASD Board of Governors.

NASD Governors recognize the contribution of Bob Bragg, Gene Lewis and Don Knutson to the securities industry with a donation of $20,000 to a newly established Continuing Education Memorial Fund in their honor.

Montana Ambassadors name Ian B. Davidson Entrepreneur of the Year.

Bob Bragg and Gene Lewis recognized and memorialized by the Montana Ambassadors.

DAD expands insurance coverage to insure all customer accounts to $10 million, up from former limit of $2.5 million.

2/10/1995 Thirty-one DADCO people receive Awards of Recognition at Great Falls dinner.

3/1995 DADCO acquires new corporate plane, a Piper Cheyenne II.

5/1995 DAD's Missoula branch moves to ground floor space in new River Front Place, downtown.

Investment Planning group, Roland, Shea & Harley joins DAD as unit of Spokane branch.

6/1995 Jack Davant named President of Financial Aims Corporation, filling vacancy created by death of Gene Lewis.

Douglas Blattmachr named President of TrustCorp, filling vacancy created by death of Bob Bragg.

7/1995 Paul Wonnacott named DAD Senior Vice President and Director of Retail Branches.

First-ever Montana meeting of NASD Board of Governors convenes in Bigfork, Montana, hosted by NASD Chairman Ian B. Davidson. Pacific Stock Exchange Board of Governors meet in Bigfork.

8/1995 Gary Buchanan joins DAD in Billings as Branch Manager and Senior Regional Vice President, Institutional Sales.

9/1995 DAD's Bozeman office moves to 529 East Main.

9/29/1995 DJIA reaches 4789.08.

Total capital exceeds $38 million. Total client assets under management reach $4.5 billion. Total employment reaches 378.

1995...

Ian B. Davidson becomes first executive from the Pacific Northwest to chair the NASD Board of Governors. Jack Davant is named President of Financial Aims Corporation. Douglas Blattmachr is named President of TrustCorp.

....

Total capital exceeds $38 million. Total client assets under management reach $4.5 billion.

10/15/95	Donn Lassila, an experienced technology specialist joins DAD in the computer area of the Operations Department.
10/95	Five DAD employees become the first recipients of Continuing Education Memorial Fund Scholarships. The Fund honors the contributions of Bob Bragg, Gene Lewis and Don Knutson to the industry.
11/1995	DAD's Great Falls retail office expands into new quarters in Davidson Building.
11/4/95	Ken Reesman named the first recipient of the Bragg/Lewis/Knutson (B/L/K) Community Service Award given annually as a tribute to those who lost their lives in the 1994 Company plane crash.

1996-2000: *Moving On*

1/1996	Ian Davidson's term as NASD Governor and 1995 Chairman expires, as does his nine years of service on the Pacific Exchange Board. L. Bruce Madsen succeeds him.
3/21-23/1996	25 Financial Consultants qualify for the initial meeting of the newly-created President's Club at the Washington Athletic Club in Seattle.
5/16/1996	Davidson Honors College, a gift from Ian and Nancy Davidson, is dedicated on the campus of U of M.

1996...

Davidson Honors College, a gift from Ian and Nancy Davidson, is dedicated on the campus of U of M.

9/1/1996	MSU–Billings, under Dr. Stacey Suydam, becomes sixth participant in the Student Investment Program which was started at MSU–Bozeman in 1985. Dr. Suydam joined DAD in 1997 as a Financial Consultant.
9/30/1996	Capital reaches $46.9 million and assets under management, $5.9 billion.
11/16/1996	Chuck McAdam is the second recipient of the B/L/K Community Service Award.
2/3/1997	Randy Yoakum joins DAD as Senior VP and Chief Investment Officer.

. . . .

Capital reaches $46.9 million and assets under management, $5.9 billion.

2/24/1997	Bob Magnuson joins DAD as Pacific Northwest Regional Director of Branches as the prelude to the development of the Seattle–Portland area.
	Daren Shaw joins Capital Markets Group in Salt Lake City as Managing Director in Corporate Finance.
7/15/1997	Joe Heffernan, Vice President and Manager of Norwest Bank in Sioux City, Iowa, joins TrustCorp as Senior Vice President and Trust Officer.
8/151997	The first DAD retail branch office in Utah is opened in Salt Lake City with W. Rex Thornton and James C. Wheeler as co-managers.
9/15/1997	Capital Investment Advisors, an independent investment management group in Boise, Idaho, joins DAD.
9/26/1997	D.A. Davidson & Co./DADCO recognized by Montana State University as Family Business of the Year in its Large Company category.
	Veteran Manager of the Great Falls branch, Bert Thurber, steps down after 10 years of service and is succeeded by Eric Gysler.
9/30/1997	Capital increases 13% to $53 million and assets under management 23.7% to $7.3 billion.
10/1/1997	TrustCorp officially becomes Davidson Trust Co. to more effectively identify its affiliation with the widely-respected Davidson name.
10/11/1997	The 1997 revision of the DADCO Strategic Plan is unveiled at the 1997 Annual Meeting. It was the sixth such revision made since 1982, and its most extensive to date.

> **1997**
>
> *D.A. Davidson & Co./ DADCO recognized by Montana State University as Family Business of the Year in its Large Company category.*

> ▪ ▪ ▪ ▪
>
> *Capital increases 13% to $53 million and assets under management 23.7% to $7.3 billion.*

| 11/28/1997 | Aberdeen, Washington, becomes 20th DAD branch office. |

| 1/23/1998 | DADCO Board is reorganized to conform to the Strategic Plan recommendation to provide increased diversity. Diane Irvine, Plum Creek CFO in Seattle, is named second outside director. |

Vinney Purpura is elected President and CEO of D.A. Davidson & Co., succeeding Ian Davidson who continues as Chairman and CEO of DADCO.

| 2/1/1998 | Acquisition of Jensen Securities, an equity research firm based in Portland, Oregon, adds 19 new research professionals to DAD's research staff. |

Bill Dezellum, Vice President and Senior Research Analyst at ICM Investment Management, joins Financial Aims as Senior Portfolio Manager.

Capital Markets Group announce a major expansion in the Seattle area with the addition of four new seasoned professionals.

| 2/23/1998 | DAD employees recognize Ian Davidson for forty years of service to DAD with a public reception. |

| 3/1998 | 21st branch office opens in Redmond, Washington, under the direction of Vice President Miles Otoupal. |

A second Spokane branch satellite is opened in the South Hill area with Paul Dumais at the helm.

A Bozeman branch satellite in Livingston, Montana, opens, headed by Jack McInerney, formerly with Edward Jones.

| 4/1998 | D.A. Davidson & Co. creates a Professional Development Department under the direction of Jim Searles as Vice President and Director. Its announced goal is to enhance the ability of DAD brokers to serve the individual investor. |

DADCO TRAVEL acquires The Travel Bug Agency, established in Missoula in 1974 by Barbara Koessler, who has joined the DADCO TRAVEL Board as a director.

DAD opens a retail branch office in Sheridan, Wyoming, with Tracy Swanson as Vice President and Manager.

5/1998   Davidson Trust Co. purchases the trust assets of Glacier Bank of Kalispell. Jeff Mahon joins DTC as Vice President and Trust Officer.

Manager Information Systems becomes a separate department under the direction of Vice President Donn Lasilla. Clay Gehring joins the department as Curriculum Coordinator.

6/1998   Client Support becomes first DAD department to move into the recently-purchased and newly-renovated Liberty Center.

Compliance Department is reorganized and expanded. Arlene Wilson, CPA, joins DADCO as Vice President and Director of Compliance.

9/1998   D.A. Davidson & Co. opens a major branch office in Portland, Oregon, with Russell W. Tennant as Vice President and Branch Manager. He is initially joined by a professional staff of four Financial Consultants and a support staff of four.

Ian and Nancy Davidson are recognized by the University of Montana with its Community Service Award at a public reception in Great Falls. The Award recognizes alumni for their service to the University as well as to the community in which they live.

10/31/1998   Stu Nicholson receives the fourth annual B/L/K Community Service Award, primarily for his contributions to the Boy Scouts of America.

> ....
>
> *Ian and Nancy Davidson are recognized by the University of Montana with its Community Service Award at a public reception in Great Falls. The Award recognizes alumni for their service to the University as well as to the community in which they live.*

| 12/4/1998 | The Davidson Court and Circle Plaza in downtown Great Falls is dedicated in a public ceremony. The Court features a skywalk which connects the Davidson Building and the Liberty Center. A large crowd attended the dedication and the public reception in the skywalk which followed. |

| 1/2/1999 | George E. Tootle, Senior Vice President of Operations with the Ohio Company in Columbus, Ohio, for the past 30 years, joins D.A. Davidson & Co. as Vice President, Director of Operations. |

| 1/15/1999 | Seattle Branch opens its first satellite office in Friday Harbor with Libby Thompson in charge. |

| 3/1999 | DADCO Board is expanded to 13 members with the election of Gerry Meyer, Senior Vice President, Marketing, and Doug Woodcock, Vice President, Institutional Equities for one and two year terms respectively. |

| 4/1999 | According to an industry study, D.A. Davidson & Co. with $57 million in total consolidated capital, ranks 96th out of 5400 U.S. brokerage firms as reported by *Institutional Investor* magazine. This figure included only the capital in the brokerage firm. |

| 5/1999 | The Butte Branch opens a satellite office in Dillon, Montana. |

....

The Davidson Court and Circle Plaza in downtown Great Falls is dedicated in a public ceremony. The Court features a skywalk which connects the Davidson Building and the Liberty Center. An estimated crowd in excess of 5,000 attended the dedication and the public reception in the skywalk which followed.

....

According to an industry study, D.A. Davidson & Co. with $57 million in total consolidated capital, ranks 96th out of 5400 U.S. brokerage firms as reported by Institutional Investor magazine. This figure included only the capital in the brokerage firm.

6/1999	Nancy and Ian Davidson are recognized by the Great Falls City Commission with its 1998 Community Liveability Award for the Davidson Court and Circle Plaza

6/1999 Nancy and Ian Davidson are recognized by the Great Falls City Commission with its 1998 Community Liveability Award for the Davidson Court and Circle Plaza

10/1999 Phelps-Woodhead, a 20 year old Spokane firm which specializes in personal service and financial expertise, joins D.A. Davidson & Co. Four professionals and three staff members currently manage about $400 million in customer assets, most of it in the Pacific Northwest.

Marc J. Dion, Chief Investment Officer with Ziegler Asset Management, joins Financial Aims as a Senior Portfolio Manager.

10/30/1999 Karen Grove, Davidson Trust Co. in Great Falls, was named 1999 winner of the Bragg/Lewis/Knutson Community Service Award.

1/2000 After a year-long search by an outside executive search committee, the Board of Directors elects Vincent M. Purpura to succeed Ian B. Davidson as President and Chief Executive Officer of DADCO. Ian continues as Chairman of the Board. A search was started for a President of D.A. Davidson & Co. to replace Vinney.

Bill Johnstone, Managing Partner at Dorsey & Whitney, a Minneapolis-based international law firm, is elected the third outside director of DADCO.

Joe Heffernan, Senior Vice President, is elected President of Davidson Trust Co. to succeed Jack Davant, who remains President and Chief Operating Officer of Financial Aims Corporation.

....

After a year-long search by an outside executive search committee, the Board of Directors elects Vincent M. Purpura to succeed Ian B. Davidson as President and Chief Executive Officer of DADCO. Ian continues as Chairman of the Board. A search was also started for a President of D.A. Davidson & Co. to replace Vinney.

2/18/2000 Bill Beaman, veteran Helena Financial Consultant and Manager, retires after 271/2 years of service, all of it with DAD.

3/2000	Everett, Washington, becomes DAD's fourth full-service office in the Seattle area and the seventh in the region. Jack Decker is the professional in charge.
4/2000	DAD opens its 33rd branch office in Bend, Oregon, with Bill Berner, Senior Vice President, as manager. It is the second full-service branch in Oregon.

For the second consecutive year, D.A. Davidson & Co. is represented among the 10 outstanding brokers in the United States in a contest sponsored by *Registered Representative* magazine. In 1998, Spokane brokers, R.C. Roland and Gary Shea were selected, and in 1999, Tim Owen, Bozeman manager, made the list. In both cases, they were selected from a list of hundreds of nominees.

Mark Semmens, recently appointed to the Board of Regents of the Montana University System, steps down as head of the Investment Banking Department and was succeeded by Doug Woodcock who becomes Director of Equity Capital Markets. Semmens will remain with the Department.

Charlie Abernathy steps down as manager of the Syndicate Department. Marge Sitzmann, lead manager of Equity Syndicate at Kirkpatrick Pettis in Omaha, succeeds him. Charlie remains active in the firm.

7/2000	Bill Johnstone, elected a director earlier in the year, becomes the 6th President of D.A. Davidson & Co. A Montana native, Johnstone brings a distinguished career in both law and the securities business to the firm.
8/2000	The Board of Directors approve a proposed change of names of three DADCO companies: DADCO, Inc. becomes Davidson Companies; Financial Aims Corporation becomes Davidson Investment Advisors; and DADCO TRAVEL becomes Davidson Travel.

2000

Bill Johnstone, elected a director earlier in the year, becomes the 6th President of D.A. Davidson & Co. A Montana native, Johnstone brings a distinguished career in both law and the securities business to the firm.

9/2000	Davidson Insurance Agency opens in Billings under the leadership of Jeffrey Taylor, an experienced insurance professional.
10/14/2000	Page Dabney, Bozeman, is selected to receive the 2000 B/L/K Community Service Award.
10/14/2000	The new logos for the Davidson Companies are unveiled at the annual meeting in Great Falls.

■ ■ ■ ■

The Board of Directors approve a proposed change of names of three DADCO companies:

DADCO, Inc. becomes Davidson Companies; Financial Aims Corporation becomes Davidson Investment Advisors; and DADCO TRAVEL becomes Davidson Travel.

D.A. Davidson & Co.
Davidson Trust Co.
Davidson Investment Advisors
Davidson Travel

D.A. Davidson & Co. member SIPC

Davidson Investment Advisors

Davidson Trust Co. WEALTH MANAGEMENT

Davidson Travel CONSULTANTS

DAVIDSON COMPANIES

GREAT FALLS, MONTANA

Ian B. Davidson
*Chairman, Davidson Companies
and D.A. Davidson & Co.*

Vincent M. Purpura
*President and
Chief Executive Officer,
Davidson Companies*

Stuart Nicholson, CPA
*Senior Vice President,
Chief Financial Officer*

David Dennis
*Vice President,
General Counsel*

Darlene Miller
*Vice President,
Communications Director*

Dan McLaughlin
*Vice President,
Director of Human Resources*

Dan Johannes
*Associate Vice President,
Flight Department Manager*

Anders Berry
Associate Counsel

LaVonne Harp
Corporate Secretary

Beth Ann Thelen
*Assistant to the President
and CEO*

Delores Landsverk
Assistant Corporate Secretary

William Preston, CLU
Exchange Editor

Debra Rhodes
Senior Graphic Designer

Jacquie Burchard
*Media and Public Relations
Coordinator*

Bruce McCracken
Facilities Manager

D.A. DAVIDSON & CO.

*CORPORATE OFFICE
GREAT FALLS*

William A. Johnstone
President

Gerald Meyer, CFP
*Senior Vice President,
Marketing, Regional Director
of Retail Branches*

Arlene Wilson
*Vice President,
Director of Compliance*

James Searles
*Vice President,
Director of
Professional Development*

Marge Sitzmann
*Vice President,
Director of Syndicate*

Erik Madsen
Vice President, Equity Trading

Gerald VanTighem
Vice President, Equity Trading

Rebecca McHugh
Vice President, Syndicate

Laurie Hicks
Associate, Sales and Marketing

Scott Haigh
Analyst, Managed Assets

Joely Foster
Administrator, Managed Assets

Lisa Haffner
Senior Compliance Examiner

Tammy Beaver
Compliance Examiner

Jason Hufford
Trading Associate

Rebecca Owen
Assistant to the President

*FIXED INCOME
CAPITAL MARKETS
GREAT FALLS*

Kreg Jones
*Senior Vice President,
Director of Capital Markets*

Robert Kelly
*Vice President,
Director of Fixed Income Trading*

Jim Palmer
*Senior Vice President,
Institutional Fixed Income Sales
Bend*

John Easley
*Vice President,
Fixed Income Trading*

Aaron Rudio
Vice President, Public Finance

Jack McLaughlin
*Vice President, Public Finance
Spokane*

Ritchie Secor
*Vice President,
Fixed Income Trading*

Dwight Funai
*Vice President,
Institutional Fixed Income Sales
Seattle*

Mary Ann Hurley
*Vice President,
Fixed Income Trading
Seattle*

Mark Froio
*Vice President,
Fixed Income Trading
Seattle*

Daniel Shull
*Vice President,
Institutional Fixed Income Sales*

Bridget Ekstrom
*Associate Vice President,
Public Finance
Bozeman*

Peter Wooldridge
Associate, Fixed Income Trading

Alouette Wadman
Associate, Fixed Income Trading

David Halling
*Institutional Fixed Income Sales
Seattle*

Crystal Vogl
Associate, Public Finance

INVESTMENT BANKING

Daren Shaw
*Managing Director
of Investment Banking
Salt Lake City*

Mark Semmens
*Managing Director
Great Falls*

Al Glowasky
*Managing Director
Portland*

Eric Peterson
*Vice President
Salt Lake City*

Jason Purpura
*Associate
Great Falls*

Tom Hayes
*Associate
Portland*

Ann Nahajski
*Associate
Seattle*

Douglas Woodcock
Vice President,
Director of Equity Capital Markets

John Rogers, CFA
Vice President, Director of Research

Bob Mitchell
Vice President,
Director of Institutional Sales

Jim Volk
Co-Director,
Institutional Trading

Dan Baker
Co-Director,
Institutional Trading

Mike Shea
Vice President,
Senior Research Analyst

Jim Bellessa, CFA
Vice President,
Senior Research Analyst
Great Falls

James Bradshaw
Vice President,
Senior Research Analyst

Steve Chercover, CFA
Vice President,
Senior Research Analyst

Gary Levine
Vice President,
Institutional Sales

Stephanie Lipman-Dagoberg
Vice President,
Sales Trading

G. Paul Willey
Vice President,
Institutional Sales

Shirish Mulherkar
Vice President,
Institutional Sales
Seattle

Bill Frerichs
Vice President,
Senior Research Analyst

Bill Montagne, Jr.
Vice President,
Institutional Sales

Teri Meyer
Vice President,
Institutional Sales

Bob Dvorsky
Vice President,
Research
Seattle

Anne Platt
Vice President,
Institutional Sales

Bob Ehlen
Vice President,
Institutional Sales

Mark Corcoran, CFA
Vice President, Research
Retail

Corey Hughes
Associate Vice President,
Senior Equity Trader

Shawn Narancich, CFA
Research Analyst

Kevin Giboney
Research Analyst
Seattle

Stephanie Fox
Portfolio Strategist

Jay Brenn
Systems Manager

Jennifer Corpe
Research Associate

Rodrigo Hulse
Equity Trader

Mike Wonsiewicz
Sales Trader

Isaac Bamer
Sales Trader

DAVIDSON INSURANCE AGENCY

Jeffrey Taylor
Vice President, Insurance
Billings

CLIENT SUPPORT
GREAT FALLS

Darrell Block, CPA
Vice President, Controller

George Tootle
Vice President,
Director of Operations

Keith Bjorsness
Vice President, Cashier

Doug Nicholson
Vice President,
Assistant Controller

Donn Lassila
Vice President, Director,
Information Technology

Greg Nagel
Vice President,
Computer Programming

Bonnie Fuller
Associate Vice President,
Cashier, Secretary

Mary Brennan-Dutro
Associate Vice President,
Treasurer

Tom Nicholson
Associate Vice President,
Assistant Cashier

Rick McDonald
Associate Vice President,
Cash Management

Linda St. Germain
Associate Vice President,
Assistant Cashier

Elaine Christensen, CPA
Associate Vice President,
Assistant Controller

Clay Gehring
Associate Vice President, IT,
Curriculum and
Training Administrator

Siama Karhi
Associate Vice President,
Account Transfers

Patrick Kafer
Associate Vice President,
Sales/Operations Liaison
Seattle

Kay Lopuch
Programmer/Analyst

Terry Kangas
Staff Accountant

Bob Brook
Special Projects Coordinator

PACIFIC EXCHANGE
SPECIALIST POSTS

CALIFORNIA

SAN FRANCISCO

Dave Hultman
Vice President,
Specialist Operations

John Podany
Vice President, Specialist

John Fritschi
Vice President, Specialist

Walter Reinsdorf
Vice President, Specialist

Brian Geary
Vice President, Options,
Lead Market Maker

Tom Stephenson
Administration

Kathleen Gallagher
Floor Broker

Jim Pringle
Network Administrator

Greg Block
Specialist

Henry Tsan
Specialist

Artie Penza
Specialist

Troy Onorato
Specialist

Jonathan Hopkins
Specialist

Bill Ryan
Lead Market Maker

Mark Bruskotter
Financial Consultant

Skip Halmes
Financial Consultant

Brad Thurber
Financial Consultant

HAMILTON

James Moerkerke, CFP
Senior Vice President+,
Financial Consultant,
Branch Manager

Lawrence "Mike" Hudson
Vice President,+
Financial Consultant

Joe Lantz
Senior Financial Consultant

Vicki Lantz
Senior Financial Consultant

HAVRE

Steve Bebee, CFP
Vice President,
Financial Consultant,
Branch Manager

Scott Wink
Vice President,
Financial Consultant

Max Erickson
Vice President,+
Financial Consultant

Gregory Dugdale, CMFC
Senior Financial Consultant

Susan LaSalle
Financial Consultant

HELENA

Kelly Kuntz
Vice President,
Financial Consultant,
Branch Manager

James Barfknecht
Vice President,
Financial Consultant,
Assistant Branch Manager

Nancy Nicholson, CFP
Vice President,+
Financial Consultant

Brent Rehm
Vice President,+
Financial Consultant

Terry Cohea
Vice President,+
Financial Consultant

Patrick Sullivan
Senior Financial Consultant

Michael Holland
Senior Financial Consultant

Dave Bauer
Senior Financial Consultant

Rob Bean
Financial Consultant

Janet Hedges
Financial Consultant

KALISPELL
WHITEFISH

Ronald Hopkins
Vice President,
Financial Consultant,
Branch Manager

Timothy Schnee
Vice President,+
Financial Consultant,
Assistant Branch Manager

Robert A. Braig
Senior Vice President,
Financial Consultant

Gregory Barkus
Senior Vice President,+
Financial Consultant

Samuel Wayman
Vice President,+
Financial Consultant

Michael Houtonen
Vice President,+
Financial Consultant

Terry Judd
Vice President,+
Financial Consultant

Rob O. Braig
Vice President,+
Financial Consultant

Ronald Matelich
Vice President,+
Financial Consultant
Whitefish

Jay Flynn
Senior Financial Consultant

Kenneth Barkus
Senior Financial Consultant

MISSOULA

Frank D'Angelo, CFP
Vice President,
Financial Consultant,
Branch Manager

Paul Eichwald
Senior Vice President,+
Financial Consultant

Nathan English
Vice President,
Financial Consultant

Ken Reesman
Vice President,+
Financial Consultant

Bruce Madsen
Vice President,+
Financial Consultant

Raymond Round
Vice President,+
Financial Consultant

Philip Perszyk
Vice President,+
Financial Consultant

Jim Huggins
Associate Vice President,+
Financial Consultant+

Timothy Kato, CLU
Associate Vice President,+
Financial Consultant

Errol Mann
Senior Financial Consultant

Jim Benson
Senior Financial Consultant

Richard Peterson
Senior Financial Consultant

Meegan Kriley
Financial Consultant

Cynthia Brenden
Financial Consultant

WYOMING
CODY

David Neihart
Financial Consultant

GILLETTE

David Jones
Vice President,
Financial Consultant,
Branch Manager

Burns "Butch" Byram III
Vice President,
Financial Consultant

Scott Barstad
Senior Financial Consultant

Candace Crow
Senior Financial Consultant

SHERIDAN

Tracy Swanson
Vice President,+
Financial Consultant

Karen Ferguson
Financial Consultant

Frank Boley
Financial Consultant

David Sanders
Financial Consultant

IDAHO
BOISE

Thomas Zemlicka
Vice President,
Financial Consultant

Craig Nern
Vice President,
Financial Consultant,
Assistant Branch Manager

Michael Cusack
Senior Vice President,+
Portfolio Manager

John McCune, CFA
Senior Vice President,+
Portfolio Manager

Michael Bledsoe, CFA
Vice President,+
Portfolio Manager

Scott Ferguson, CFA
Vice President,+
Financial Consultant

James Wolfe
Vice President,+
Financial Consultant

James Ripley
Financial Consultant

John Corddry
Financial Consultant

Edelene Ceynar Ohman
Financial Consultant

Coeur d'Alene
Sandpoint

Cort Wilcox
Vice President,
Financial Consultant,
Branch Manager

Bradley Dugdale
Senior Vice President,+
Financial Consultant

Mark Bowlby
Senior Vice President,+
Financial Consultant

Thomas Gibson, CPA
Vice President,+
Financial Consultant
Sandpoint

Kevin Glynn
Associate Vice President,+
Financial Consultant

Catherine Kleinhans
Senior Financial Consultant

Richard Ronnestad
Financial Consultant

Mara'd Sjostrom
Financial Consultant

Rick Shenfield
Financial Consultant

Bill Waggoner
Financial Consultant

Lori Grasham
Financial Consultant

Lewiston
Moscow

Jeffrey Nesset, CFP
Vice President,
Financial Consultant,
Branch Manager

Richard Rognas
Vice President,+
Financial Consultant

Thomas Richardson
Vice President,+
Financial Consultant
Moscow

Robert Blakey
Vice President,+
Financial Consultant

Rick Pegram
Vice President,+
Financial Consultant

A.C. "Bud" Nelson, Jr.
Associate Vice President,+
Financial Consultant

Charlie Truksa
Senior Financial Consultant

William Goesling, Ph.D.
Senior Financial Consultant,
Moscow

JoAnn Evans
Financial Consultant
Moscow

Scott Baldwin
Financial Consultant

WASHINGTON

Aberdeen

Edwin Klein
Senior Vice President,+
Financial Consultant,
Branch Manager

Charles Vammen
Vice President,+
Financial Consultant

Dave Beard
Vice President,+
Financial Consultant

Steven Levold
Associate Vice President,+
Financial Consultant

Jeremy Hawkins
Financial Consultant

Pullman

Kay Bundy
Associate Vice President,+
Financial Consultant

Judi Shipley
Financial Consultant

Redmond

Miles Otoupal
Vice President,
Financial Consultant,
Branch Manager

Russell Van Moppes
Senior Vice President,+
Financial Consultant

Michael Bell
Senior Vice President,+
Financial Consultant

Donald Clough
Senior Vice President,+
Financial Consultant

Alan Worden
Vice President,+
Financial Consultant

Brenda Berg
Vice President,+
Financial Consultant

Brian Orton
Vice President,+
Financial Consultant

Michael Bell, Jr.
Senior Financial Consultant

M. Lynn Van Moppes
Financial Consultant

Michael Wagner
Financial Consultant

Seattle
Friday Harbor
Everett

Robert Magnuson
Senior Vice President,
Regional Director
of Retail Branches

Paul Fahey
Vice President,
Financial Consultant,
Branch Manager

John Bender
Vice President,+
Financial Consultant,
Assistant Manager

Theodore Pappas
Senior Vice President,+
Financial Consultant

John "Greg" Fenton
Senior Vice President,+
Financial Consultant

Dwayne Berg
Senior Vice President+,
Financial Consultant

Heath McHenry
Senior Vice President,+
Financial Consultant

David Karpan
Senior Vice President,+
Financial Consultant

Douglas Nichols
Senior Vice President,+
Financial Consultant

Michael Morrison
Senior Vice President,+
Financial Consultant

Scott Lisle
Senior Vice President,+
Financial Consultant

James Perry
Senior Vice President,+
Financial Consultant

Rick Shelby
Senior Vice President,+
Financial Consultant

Jack Decker
Senior Vice President,+
Financial Consultant
Everett

John Fagan
Senior Vice President,+
Financial Consultant
Everett

Libby Thompson
Vice President,+
Financial Consultant
Friday Harbor

Bill Greenfield
Vice President,+
Financial Consultant
Friday Harbor

Jeff Decker
Vice President,+
Financial Consultant
Everett

Taeya Lauer
Financial Consultant

Jerry Low
Financial Consultant

Khoi Cung
Financial Consultant

Casey Shurm
Financial Consultant

Marty Healey
Financial Consultant

SPOKANE
SOUTH HILL

Robert Cummings
Vice President,
Financial Consultant,
Branch Manager

David Milbrath
Senior Vice President,+
Financial Consultant

R.C. Roland
Senior Vice President,+
Financial Consultant

Garry Shea
Senior Vice President,+
Financial Consultant

John Woodhead
Senior Vice President,+
Financial Consultant

Eric Allen
Senior Vice President,+
Financial Consultant

Michael Dix
Vice President,+
Financial Consultant

Glenn Baldwin
Vice President,+
Financial Consultant

Douglas Dumais
Vice President,+
Financial Consultant

Kirt Fredericks
Vice President,+
Financial Consultant

Paul Dumais
Vice President,+
Financial Consultant
South Hill

Grant Marks
Vice President,+
Financial Consultant
South Hill

John Woodhead, Jr.
Vice President,+
Financial Consultant

Gary Douvia
Vice President,+
Financial Consultant

Michael Shea
Associate Vice President,+
Financial Consultant

Molly K. Harley
Associate Vice President,+
Financial Consultant

Kathy Bott
Associate Vice President,
Operations Manager,
Registered Associate

Jody Stewart
Associate Vice President,
Registered Associate

Merilee Frets
Financial Consultant
South Hill

Terence Anderson
Financial Consultant

Monte Chitwood
Financial Consultant

Larry Thompson
Financial Consultant

Chad Roland
Financial Consultant

WENATCHEE

Robert Johnson II
Senior Vice President,+
Financial Consultant,
Branch Manager

UTAH
SALT LAKE CITY

W. Rex Thornton, CFP, CPA
Senior Vice President,+
Financial Consultant,
Co-Manager

Jim Wheeler
Senior Vice President,+
Financial Consultant,
Co-Manager

Ken Hansen
Senior Vice President,+
Financial Consultant

Brad Hansen
Senior Vice President,+
Financial Consultant

T.J. Bugger
Associate Vice President,+
Financial Consultant

Paul Hansen
Financial Consultant

Craig Schultz
Financial Consultant

OREGON
PORTLAND

Russell Tennant
Vice President,
Financial Consultant,
Branch Manager

Betsy Russell
Senior Vice President,+
Financial Consultant

Dennis Lowenthal
Senior Vice President,+
Financial Consultant

Cynthia Burg
Senior Vice President,+
Financial Consultant

Wade Peterson
Vice President,+
Financial Consultant

Richard Thomas
Vice President,+
Financial Consultant

BEND

Bill Berner
Senior Vice President,+
Financial Consultant,
Branch Manager

+This title is an honorary title given to those who have excelled in customer service and have vast experience in the securities industry.
Member SIPC, Pacific Exchange, Boston and Chicago Exchanges.